OXFORD
INDIA SHORT
INTRODUCTIONS
PATHWAYS TO
ECONOMIC
DEVELOPMENT

The Oxford India Short
Introductions are concise,
stimulating, and accessible guides
to different aspects of India.
Combining authoritative analysis,
new ideas, and diverse perspectives,
they discuss subjects which are
topical yet enduring, as also
emerging areas of study and debate.

OTHER TITLES IN THE SERIES

Mughal Painting
Som Prakash Verma

Coalition Politics in India
Bidyut Chakrabarty

Political Economy of Reforms in India
Rahul Mukherji

Dalit Assertion
Sudha Pai

The Civil Services in India
S.K. Das

Affirmative Action in India
Ashwini Deshpande

The Right to Information in India
Sudhir Naib

Water Resources of India
A. Vaidyanathan

Panchayati Raj
Kuldeep Mathur

Caste
Surinder S. Jodhka

For more information visit our website:
http://www.oup.co.in/section/academic-general

A part of the *Oxford India Short Introductions* series, this book belongs to a cluster of nine titles around the theme 'Economics and Development'. I have deliberately kept these two words separate. We tend to forget that the non-economic aspects of development have an important bearing on the economic aspects. The focus of the theme is how a country like India faces and solves (or fails to solve) various questions related to its quest for sustainable development. Moreover, every book within this cluster presents the reader with a quick recapitulation of the relevant theory so that opinions can be disentangled from conclusions based on theory.

Anindya Sen, Professor of Economics, Indian Institute of Management Calcutta; General Editor for the cluster on 'Economics and Development', *OISI*

Other Titles in the Cluster

International Trade and India
Parthapratim Pal

Capital Flows and Exchange Rate Management
Soumyen Sikdar

Trade and Environment
Rajat Acharyya

Monetary Policy
Partha Ray

Indian Cities
Annapurna Shaw

OXFORD
INDIA SHORT
INTRODUCTIONS

PATHWAYS TO ECONOMIC DEVELOPMENT

AMITAVA KRISHNA DUTT

OXFORD
UNIVERSITY PRESS

OXFORD
UNIVERSITY PRESS

Oxford University Press is a department of the University of Oxford.
It furthers the University's objective of excellence in research, scholarship,
and education by publishing worldwide. Oxford is a registered trademark of
Oxford University Press in the UK and in certain other countries

Published in India by
Oxford University Press
YMCA Library Building, 1 Jai Singh Road, New Delhi 110 001, India

ISBN-13: 978-0-19-807539-4
ISBN-10: 0-19-807539-1

Typeset in 11/15.6 Bembo Std
by Excellent Laser Typesetters, Pitampura, Delhi 110 034
Printed in India at G.H. Prints Pvt Ltd, New Delhi 110 020

For Arnav,
with the hope that he and his generation
will take the right paths

Contents

Tables and Figures

Tables

Figures

Preface

This book is the result of many years of thinking, reading, writing, and teaching about economic development. During these years I have incurred many debts. I should thank students at the University of Notre Dame, especially those in the Minor in International Development Studies, and at FLACSO, Ecuador, for discussing many development issues with me and for helping me to formulate many of the ideas presented in the book. Many friends and colleagues have influenced my thinking about the ideas discussed in the book, and some have provided comments and encouragement in the course of writing it. Anindya Sen has been particularly generous with his comments on several drafts, and Amiya Bagchi, Lance Taylor, and Tony Thirlwall have been very encouraging. The comments of three anonymous referees for Oxford University Press have helped to improve the book's content and presentation, although they have not always agreed with my views and emphases. Research assistance from Avirup Dutt and Jamie Long is gratefully acknowledged. I should thank the editorial team of Oxford University Press for their patience and encouragement. Finally, my families in India and the US, and especially Harolyn and Arnav, and our pet, Cora, have helped in many ways, not the least by creating an environment in which I could enjoy writing the book.

Since the book is meant to be a short introduction, it is addressed primarily to the interested general reader and to students and scholars approaching development studies and development economics for the first time. However, I hope my colleagues in economics and political science will find some of it of some interest to them. To keep the text brief and uncluttered, I have abstained from providing references to many of the claims I have made or summarized in the book. The interested reader is referred to the readings listed at the end of the book for more details.

1

Introduction

India's per capita income was about Rs 64,000 (for 2010),[1] which translates into approximately US$1,400.[2] This is considerably lower than those of the US (US$47,000) and Japan (US$43,000), or even Mexico (US$9,100), Brazil (US$10,700), and China (US$4,400), and is closer to the average for Ghana and Sudan. India is ranked 138 out of 190 countries listed by the World Bank. Since most things that people buy are cheaper in India, with reference to prices in the US, a US dollar can buy more in India than in the US. If

[1] All data in the book pertains to the year 2010, unless specified otherwise.

[2] Towards the end of March 2014, when this book was prepared for the press, US$1 was roughly equal to Rs 60.

we convert rupees into Purchasing Power Parity (or PPP) dollars to take this into account, India's per capita income is US$3,400, compared with $47,310 for the US, $34,600 for Japan, $14,400 for Mexico, $11,000 for Brazil, and $7,640 for China, and closer to those for Guyana and Vietnam. India ranks 126 out of 181 listed countries.

Countries with low average levels of production and income such as India are usually described as less developed, underdeveloped, developing, or economically poor countries. They are less developed not just in terms of average income, but also in terms of literacy rates, life expectancy at birth, and child mortality, as we shall see later. Beyond numbers, even a cursory examination of living and working conditions of most of the people in India's cities and villages reveals the huge difference in levels of economic prosperity between rich countries and countries like India (though there are vast differences in conditions for different people in both sets of countries as well).

This book will provide a short introduction to the pathways available to less developed countries (henceforth LDCs for short), such as India, for becoming more economically developed. For the most part, it will examine general conceptual and analytical issues, and also illustrate them with reference to the case of India and, to a lesser extent, other relevant countries.

The paths to development are neither obvious nor easy. If they were, perhaps, there would not be any LDCs. There are many academic, policy, and popular debates about whether there is a magical path to development that is available for all places and times, about what that path looks like and, more reasonably, whether there are optimal or even workable paths for specific times and places. To provide a flavour of these debates, we briefly mention some that attract a great deal of attention.

1. What should the role of the state be in development? Should it actively promote development? Or is the state the problem and not the solution, and development best left to private initiative and free markets?

2. Should countries try to increase their inter-actions with the rest of the world, that is, go global, or should they focus more within their borders and delink from the rest of the world?

3

3. Should countries promote growth over other objectives, should they focus on poverty and what are sometimes called social indicators such as those related to health and education, or should they reduce income inequality?

4. Should development efforts in a country be concentrated on a particular sector of the economy, whether broad ones such as agriculture, manufacturing, or services? Or should they be concentrated on some narrower sectors, like heavy or basic industries, or technologically simple manufacturing sectors?

5. Should countries concentrate on increasing the supply of resources, goods, and services or should they try to increase the demand for the same?

6. Should the focus be on the micro level of individuals and small communities, or should it be on the broad sectoral, economy-wide, or macro levels?

7. Should countries focus on increasing the amount of resources such as capital and labour or increase the efficiency and utilization of these resources?

8. Should countries concentrate on creating the right institutions—what may be called the rules of the game—and if so, what are they? Or should they try to overcome problems with appropriate policy prescriptions that directly affect the behaviour of individuals and groups, without worrying primarily about institutions?

Three aspects should be noted regarding these questions. One, they do not provide a comprehensive list, but reflect only some of the more important debates. For instance, another issue which has been debated is whether small or large organizations—industrial firms and agricultural farms, for example—are best for development. Two, although some of them may seem to be closely related and often are in actual debates, they are conceptually distinct. For instance, those who favour minimal government intervention in the economy also want to remove government restrictions on imports and foreign capital inflows and, therefore, favour globalization. However, greater export openness may require greater, rather than lesser, government intervention, in the form of active government assistance to exporting industries, including initial protection from foreign competitors. Three, it will probably come as no surprise—at least to those familiar with the ideas of the Buddha and Aristotle—that extreme positions on these questions are misguided, and the best option is to follow a middle path. Yet, it is useful to focus on extreme views because the debates are often waged in extreme forms. Moreover, a discussion of the extremes is illuminating for understanding why they are problematic, why some of them are not really opposites, and for providing guidance on how to find the right middle ground in specific conditions.

Answers to the questions just posed obviously depend on what we mean by development. Chapter 2 will examine the meaning and measurement of development. Although development is often conceptualized and measured in terms of average real income (as we have in the opening paragraph of this chapter) and the pace of development is usually measured by the rate of growth of per capita income, that chapter will argue that this measure, although useful, misses a great deal and discuss alternative concept and measures. In addition to this, Chapter 2 will briefly examine how well India is doing in terms of these concepts.

To analyse the issues posed by these questions, we then proceed by discussing the major obstacles to development to explain why poor countries are poor and examine examples of policies for overcoming these obstacles. Chapter 3 will explore the main obstacles that have been emphasized in narrow economic discussions, arising from factors internal to a country and Chapter 4 will turn to those factors which are related to economic relations between the country and the rest of the world and which emphasize the role of the country in the global economy. Chapter 5 will take a broader perspective, focusing on obstacles arising from social, political, cultural, and geographical factors, as well as what have been called institutional ones. The obstacles to development, as may be expected, are many, and our discussion will focus on issues that are particularly relevant to the Indian and similar contexts. Chapter 6 will then return to the debates on pathways to development to address the questions and issues regarding alternative strategies of development, and briefly appraise the paths taken by India and some other countries in the past and at present. Chapter 7 will furnish some concluding remarks.

The approach we adopt here to analyse the pathways to development—focusing on a number of debates on alternative strategies which attempt to overcome some of the major obstacles to development—is not the only way of examining different paths. An alternative is to examine the development experiences of particular countries—those which have developed successfully and those which have not—for instance, the US, Japanese, Chinese, and Ugandan paths, to draw lessons from their experiences. Yet another way is to distinguish between alternative strategies or 'models' which recommend the use of different configurations of policies, such as neo-liberal, heavy-industry first, growth-with-redistribution, and socialist strategies. While these methods might have some uses for this short introduction, they can turn our attention to debates about what a country actually did (and how what it did may have changed over time), what the composite strategies really comprise of, and whether they truly are alternatives.

Some further thoughts may be presented. First, how should we study in greater detail the problems of, and solutions to, poverty and the lack of development? What are the appropriate methods? Should we use mathematical models, statistical techniques, historical analyses, and case studies drawing on actual experiences in LDCs? Although questions regarding method are not examined at length in this book in order to focus on more substantive issues, they are not unimportant, and Chapter 7, among other things, will briefly comment on them.

Second, in examining development, why focus on *economic* development? What is signified by the term 'economic'? Doesn't 'development' also depend on other factors, including what we may call the social, the political, and the psychological? As we will see in the next chapter, we do it to narrow the scope of our analysis and avoid addressing distracting controversies. However, we will not discuss development on narrow 'economic' terms either, broadening our analysis, especially in Chapter 5.

Third, is economic development a *good* thing? Some scholars of development have questioned whether it really is. They have argued that what they call the 'development project' is a means of socially constructing differences between the superior people and nations who are perceived as being developed and the inferior, underdeveloped ones, and this allows development experts to teach the 'other' to learn from them and follow their footsteps on the trails they have blazed (Escobar 2011). They have also pointed to many instances in which expert advice and action in the name of development has produced disastrous consequences. There is much that is valid in what these critics argue, and it is advisable to be aware of their admonitions. Nevertheless, the criticisms arguably apply to particular conceptions of, and paths to, development, as we will discuss in the next chapter, and not to the idea of improvement itself. Starvation, disease, and other forms of misery and suffering in many parts of the world is real, not entirely or even largely imagined, and carefully interpreted and implemented, economic development can seek to reduce them.

We conclude with the acknowledgement that a short book such as this cannot even begin to provide a thorough survey of development economics, to cover its theories, empirics, and broad strategies and policies. Readers who want detailed coverage can consult a wide range of sources. They may start with short recent reviews of some of the main issues in development economics in Dutt and Ros (2008) and Thirlwall's (2011) balanced and comprehensive textbook-treatment of the subject. Those who are in search of analytical treatments using mathematics can consult Ray (2011) for a broad mainstream neoclassical perspective and Taylor (1983) for what can be called a heterodox structuralist perspective. This volume concentrates on some key ideas and concepts, and the main debates about strategies, with some personal (I hope, acceptable) opinions mixed in.

2

Meaning and Measurement of Development

What does development mean and how can we measure it? Presumably, it refers to something good, to some sort of improvement. Although, as noted in the previous chapter, there are critics of the 'development project' because of its allegedly misguided application of western concepts such as 'modernization' to other societies, these reservations arguably relate to some specific conceptions of development, rather than to the idea of improvements in any sense. But these criticisms also point to some of the complexities involved in conceptualizing development.

These complexities can be understood in terms of some preliminary questions. First, what is the appropriate *unit* for which we ought to examine development?

For individual people, groups of people, for inanimate objects, and conceptual systems like a nation? Second, since development implies improvement, in terms of what indices or measures or in what spaces should we conceptualize it—in terms of single indices such as income and production, utility (that is, how people feel), or some combination of measures? Third, should we confine ourselves to what actually happens, or outcomes, or also in terms of some characteristics of people and societies—such as laws or the way the society is organized? That is, should we follow what ethicists call a consequentialist or a deontological approach? Fourth, according to whom should we evaluate whether improvements are occurring? According to the individuals, groups of people, or entire societies undergoing it, or according to impartial observers or development experts? Fifth, what is the appropriate domain of development? Should we look at a variety of factors, say the social, political, and psychological, among others, or focus only the 'economic' and, if so, what is included in that term? Finally, is development an end in itself or a means to something else? Much of the literature conceptualizes development as intrinsically good, as an end in itself, while recognizing that many aspects of development may be instrumentally good as well, a means to other aspects of development.

Income, Production, and Growth

We may start with the most widely used indicator of development, that is, levels and growth rates of income and production. Figures for individuals relate to the income received by an individual. Aggregate figures typically measure the market value of all final goods and services produced (which is roughly equal to total income). Since the aggregates depend on the size of the country in terms of population, they are divided by population to obtain per capita figures, and to abstract from the effects of changes in prices (or inflation), they are measured in constant prices or real terms. Comparisons across countries are made using what are called Purchasing Power Parity (PPP) values to take into account the fact that what people buy costs different amounts in different countries when expressed in terms of a common currency using actual exchange rates. Five hundred rupees, for instance, will buy someone more, on average, in India than in the US (where it is less than US$20 when converted at the exchange rate) because the prices of many things in the US—for instance, food in similar restaurants, and services such as haircuts—are higher than they are in India (although, internationally, traded goods such as shirts are closer in price).

Production and income can be taken to show how well a person or a country as a whole is doing. If people receive more income or produce more, they can obtain more goods and services and therefore have the possibility of having a higher standard of living or well-being in some sense. However, though income and production provide people and countries with the means of becoming better off, they do not imply that they are actually better off. Thus, increases in per capita income and its growth can be taken to be instrumentally good, but not intrinsically so. However, this approach can be justified in a number of ways. One invokes the argument that individuals prefer, and feel better by, having more goods and services. Thus, when income and production increase, they are better off by their own reckoning, which implies an intrinsic improvement. Most mainstream (often called neoclassical) economists take this approach, assuming that individuals have given preferences which reflect their subjective feelings (or utility), that they obtain higher utility when they obtain more of any good or service, and that they maximize their utility. A second relates to the idea that if people and countries have higher levels of income, they have more resources, which allows them to obtain what they have reason to value, such as better education, better health, and better environmental conditions. A third relates to the idea that countries which produce more have greater economic and productive power, which may be intrinsically desirable for the country as a whole. This last justification is related not only to per capita income and production, but also to total production, and perhaps to internationally comparable currency measures rather than PPP measures, since productivity and power arguably relate to the value of goods and services produced at world prices rather than in terms of domestic purchasing power. The first two justifications, as we shall see, are related to two other indices of development.

The approach has some obvious advantages, which explain why it is so widely used. Statistics on measures such as per capita gross national product (GNP), per capita gross domestic product (GDP), and per capita national income have been regularly collected over a long period of time (for a variety of reasons, including for tax purposes) and are widely available. Appropriately measured, the numbers can be compared across time and space, which means that we can use them to say whether a country or people are undergoing development or not, and whether one country is more developed than another. Moreover, the concept is appealing both to those who want development to refer to something people value in a 'subjective' sense (given the relation between it and individual preferences), and to those who want an 'objective' measure in terms of physical units and market prices.

Despite its widespread use, however, the approach has a number of flaws which make it problematic as an index of development. Some major problems include the following. For one, income and production may not accurately represent the amount of useful goods and services produced. They may be underestimated because the figures typically do not include the goods and services which are produced at home for consumption, such as cooking, cleaning, and childcare, often provided by women (although attempts are made to include food produced for self-consumption in family farms). They may be overestimated because some goods and services produced, such as those purchased by the government, may imply government waste and inefficiency, and other purchases by consumers may merely be the result of manipulation through sales promotion activities of firms which provide little or no satisfaction, and others may reflect natural resource depletion (for instance, the 'production' of oil). Further, the amount of goods and services is not the only thing that is relevant for the well-being of people: the utility obtained by people may depend on the amount of leisure they enjoy, on the quality of natural environment (for instance, whether the air they breathe is clean and whether their health suffers because of water and air pollution), and other aspects of society. Also, average income and production do not show how the average is distributed across people. This problem afflicts average measures for a country, and not individual measures, although it can also affect measures for households by neglecting to take into account distribution within households. In addition, how production and income translate into well-being as ends—whether in terms of utility or in terms of objective indicators such as health conditions and the availability of education and transport facilities—can vary across people, over time, and from place to place. For instance, the amount of goods and services people may need to survive with good health may depend on general health conditions (if they live in regions in which such conditions are poor and where they are subject to health hazards they may need more medicines than people who live in healthier places) and whether these goods are provided by the government (for instance, governments can supply education and health care in some places). The amount of income people need to maintain their dignity or self-respect may well vary across time and space depending on what consumption norms prevail, which in turn may depend on average consumption levels.

Given these problems, it is not surprising that empirical work on subjective well-being or happiness has not found a strong positive relation between per capita income and happiness in countries over time, and across countries, except at low levels of income (contradicting the notion that more is better), nor is there a one-to-one relation between per capita income and other objective indicators like health conditions (there being wide differences in these indicators across countries at the same level of income).

Finally, the approach can be said to be purely consequentialist, focusing on what is actually produced or received, rather than on whether people are vulnerable (due to the fragility of conditions which yield output and income) and whether they have rights and freedoms of various kinds.

On a note of caution, the easy availability of statistics can make us forget that they often do not accurately measure what they claim to measure, since the numbers are sometimes imputed in rather arbitrary and possibly biased ways, for instance, due to the under-reporting of individual incomes, the exaggeration of total production, problems with data based on surveys, and the paucity and inaccuracy of price data.

Utility and Happiness

Why not conceptualize development directly in terms of the utility that people obtain? Indeed, as noted earlier, mainstream economists usually appraise economic conditions in terms of utility levels. According to their approach, a person is better off if he or she obtains a higher level of utility according to his or her own preferences, and a society is better off if the level of utility of at least one person increases without anyone else experiencing a reduction in utility. A society is in a good state—an efficient or Pareto-optimal one—if it is not possible to obtain a higher level of utility for one person without reducing the level of utility of some other person.

It seems reasonable to follow this approach. It evaluates development according to what people prefer and how they feel, that is, according to their own reckoning. It also takes into account not only the income people receive and the goods and services they consume, but all things that make people better off, including the amount of leisure they enjoy and the state of the natural environment.

One immediate problem is that of finding out how people really feel and whether they are feeling better off or worse off. A large amount of survey data which asks people questions of the form, 'All things considered, on a scale of 1 to 10, how happy do you feel with your life?', now exists, mostly for more developed countries, and increasingly, for LDCs as well. Although not as easily and regularly available as income and production data—the figures come from surveys involving relatively small samples—there have been calls for the more systematic collection of 'happiness' or 'subjective well-being' data, and for their greater use for evaluating development.

The approach has a number of additional short-comings. There is no obvious way to aggregate the measured happiness levels of individuals, since even if one person's stated level of subjective well-being may be compared at different points in time, the levels for different people cannot be compared. Although it is possible to compare states in which some people are better off and no one is worse off, since many real-world changes involve gainers and losers, aggregation becomes necessary, and average levels of happiness are misleading. Cultural differences between people in different countries (for instance, whether they believe it is acceptable to state how happy they are, and what they mean by happiness) make it difficult to compare happiness levels across countries. It is also conceptually very difficult to know what exactly is being measured by these numbers and whether they truly represent people's well-being as reckoned by themselves. People have been known to give different responses depending on the general conditions prevailing when they are asked (whether the day is sunny or cloudy), on precisely how the questions are put, and how adapted they are to their individual conditions. The issue regarding adaptation is particularly problematic because if people who are poor adapt to their condition and 'accept' their lot, they are likely to be content, perhaps even more so than people who are in far less impoverished circumstances (according to more 'objective' measures).

People may not have enough information to be good judges of their conditions: People with poor health conditions may be happy about their health, because they are not trained to assess their health conditions in a more informed manner. Moreover, which people should be taken into account? Only those existing now or also future generations when there is reason to believe that what happens now (for instance, what happens to the natural environment) can affect people who are not yet born? Finally, the approach does not take into account that fact that groups of people can collectively value certain things and conditions in ways which are not captured by individual feelings.

Functionings and Capabilities

The problems associated with the approaches discussed so far have induced some development scholars and ethicists, most notably, Amartya Sen, to focus on achieving something and having things that people value and have reason to value, such as being educated, being healthy, not going hungry, and having dignity and self-respect. The term 'functionings' is used to refer to what extent people achieve things and conditions that are considered to be valuable, and the term 'capabilities' to the ability of people to achieve these functionings, rather than to actually achieving them. An argument in favour of capabilities as against functionings is that it is important for people to have the substantive freedom to achieve certain things, rather than being forced to achieve it if they voluntarily choose not to do so (for instance, it is important for people to have the real choice of getting adequate nutrition, and not to actually get it if they choose to diet or even fast for religious, political, or health reasons). However, since it is conceptually difficult to ascertain when people's choices are 'truly' voluntary (for instance, an alcoholic who chooses to drink), and it is harder to measure capabilities than actual functionings, the latter may be preferred for many applications.

The approach is preferable to the income and production approach because it focuses on the ends and not the means of development, that is, on intrinsically valuable things, and it evaluates what is good in terms of more objective concepts rather than subjective feelings which are subject to adaptation.

There are, however, a number of problems with this approach. First, what are appropriate functionings and capabilities? Some argue that there are some universal goods that should be included while others believe that the list should be chosen by societies, or even individuals. If we take the individual perspective, clearly not everything every individual values can be included in a list. But then how do we decide what will be included and what will not without running into the problems encountered for the utility approach? Sen has argued for the need of careful and impartial reasoning and public deliberation to resolve these issues, or at least to narrow differences in points of view, and perhaps we have to be content with this despite possible problems related to asymmetries in power and influence. Second, when we have decided what to include and how, how do we aggregate over them to represent them with a single number? There are ways of arriving at some numbers. The widely used human development index (HDI), in fact, aggregates over three elements—income (after taking its logarithm to make its value rise at a diminishing rate with income), education, and health—by giving equal weight to each in a way that many find more useful than focusing only on income. Also, aggregation may not be necessary: we may focus on the achievement of a set of basic needs, as advocated by the basic needs approach that emerged in the 1970s, looking separately at things such as education, health, and nutrition. Third, this approach raises distributional problems when we look at averages such as years of schooling, which does not take into account how the rich and poor and men and women are doing, in terms of this functioning. However, the approach can be used to examine such distributional issues in ways that may be superior to the income and production approach in some senses. Finally, there are certain goods, like freedoms, rights, and the natural environment, which are difficult to reduce to the functionings and capabilities of individuals in a simple manner (even though the capabilities approach provides a way of characterizing a range of freedoms). This is because the goods relate to procedures rather than outcomes and/or because the unit for which development is examined is not the individual, but rather collectivities such as countries.

Distributional Issues

Even if we are interested in evaluating how individuals are doing, it is not practical to keep track of how every single person is faring, since doing so would require us to gather and process too much information. Thus, evaluations are often made in terms of averages for a country, like per capita income or product, the average level of subjective well-being, the average years of schooling, and the mortality rate. However, such average figures conceal important and relevant information about how *different* people in a country are doing. For instance, average per capita income and product may be going up in a country even when the richest among the population are experiencing higher incomes while the great majority of people are receiving no gain or even lower levels of income. Also, it is possible that the average years of schooling in a country is going up while some groups of people, for instance, women, are experiencing little or no improvement in this regard. Thus, if we are concerned with the development of people we need to go beyond average figures for a country and examine how the variable is distributed. Alternatively, if we are interested in whether a country is developing, we may be interested in the extent and changes in inequality within it, if we take the view that inequality is a bad thing.

One way to address distributional issues is by examining how well the worst-off in a country or group are doing. For instance, we may want to know whether the people with the lowest levels of income are able to at least achieve some minimal level of consumption necessary for meeting basic subsistence. This level, usually called the poverty line, is difficult or even impossible to define precisely, so that different levels are used, for instance, US$1, US$2, and US$5 a day, adjusting for purchasing power differences across time and place, and national governments use their own definitions. For a given poverty line, one can count the number of people (or families) who are poor and calculate the poverty rate as the total number who are poor as a ratio of total population. We may take a decline in the poverty rate of a country as showing that development is taking place. We can also look at the worst off in terms of other concepts, such as education and health conditions, and examine whether their conditions are improving. The focus on the poor can be justified—if it is not obvious—in terms of sympathy for the deprived (perhaps motivated by religious considerations), in terms of impartiality, or in terms of the philosopher John Rawls's influential difference principle. This principle follows from the idea that individuals, under a veil of ignorance where they do not know their positions in the economic hierarchy, will be led by self-interest to adopt an arrangement of society in which the resource position (in a broad sense) of the worst-off individuals will be made as high as possible because each individual realizes that he or she can be in that position.

Another approach to the problem is to take into account inequality of income or other measures such as functionings and capabilities. Inequality of income, for instance, is often measured by the Gini coefficient which is based on the average difference between the incomes of every pair of individuals in the country, and is related to the Lorenz curve, which shows what percentage of total income is received by what per cent of the population. A country which experiences a decline in inequality can be said to be developing, other things constant. However, some ethical philosophers take the view that equality of income or resources is not necessarily a desirable goal, since it does not take into account the different contributions that people make to society, or reward greater effort or better choices of people. Arguably, however, in an uncertain world in which the effects of choices and actions are not predictable, existing levels of inequality are unlikely to be justifiable by such factors; indeed, luck—including one's social position at birth—and the configuration of social, economic, and political power have an important role to play in determining inequality. Nevertheless, these arguments do suggest that fairness and equality of outcomes need not necessarily go hand in hand, and some have been led to giving greater importance to absolute poverty than to equality. However, since we may be interested in absolute levels of functionings and capabilities, and not just in incomes, and since the former may well depend on relative income (for instance, one's dignity may depend on what one is able to consume in relation to accepted social norms which are related to average incomes), concerns about absolutes in terms of capabilities and inequality in terms of income may be closely related.

Another aspect of inequality which is relevant for development is how much inequality there is in terms of a metric like income or educational attainment for different types of people distinguished by some other characteristic, such as religion, ethnicity, gender, or place of residence (different regions of the country such as states or in urban versus rural areas); or caste, of obvious importance for India. This kind of inequality, sometimes called horizontal inequality to distinguish it from vertical inequality which refers to, for instance, how income is distributed among income groups, is particularly problematic because it is much more difficult to justify it in terms of differences in choices and effort, and often is the result of overt discriminatory practices by individuals and groups, sometimes through government actions.

Collective Goods, Rights, and Freedoms

Most of the approaches to development discussed so far can all be thought of as conceptualizing development in individualistic terms, either by looking at how individuals are doing on an average, or by taking into account how they are doing relative to others. However, development can also be thought of in collective terms and, indeed, some conceptions of development cannot be reduced to the individual level both with regard to for whom and according to whom.

On the question of for whom or for what, the full meaning and significance of many 'goods' cannot be fully captured in terms of how they affect individuals. Only groups of people can have sovereignty or the ability to govern themselves in an agreed upon manner, which can be referred to as collective capabilities. Moreover, in talking about the natural environment, one needs to go beyond humans to include other animals and trees and inanimate objects such as water, soil, and air and, in fact, the entire ecological system. Groups or countries can have laws and practices which provide rights and freedoms because by their very nature, at least in principle, they apply to everyone and, as noted earlier, one can also think of equality and inequality as the attributes of societies. Although, obviously, individuals can enjoy rights and freedoms, be unhappy about being unequally treated without good reason, and be happy if they enjoy sovereignty and clean air, in some respects, it can be argued that the ethical status of these goods cannot be reduced to the individual level.

On the question of according to whom, it is taken as self-evident by some people that individuals are the ones who decide what development means, since who else can? Thus, utility reflects people's own desires, and more income is valuable if it gets them more of what they want, and better health and education is valued only because individuals take the view that it is valuable. In the case of what economists call public goods, such as national defence, which can be provided only to groups without excluding people and which can be enjoyed by all at the same time without reducing the enjoyment of others, individuals can have personal preferences for them. However, although the individualistic approach in this sense is sensible and appealing for certain types of goods, it raises important questions for other goods. Goods such as better health and education are valuable not only because individuals may take them to be so, but also because we have reason to take them to be so. Both the words 'we' and 'reason' in the preceding sentence are important. While for individual preferences there may be no necessary social aspect (though, of course, these preferences may be affected by social factors), decisions at the social level are of a social or collective nature, since they have to be agreed to—though not unanimously or even through some clear voting procedure—through social interactions and on the basis of shared understandings and values. So-called experts from different fields (like health, education, and economics) can have a role in these deliberations, although it should be kept in mind that experts can have their own biases and vested interests, and often have disproportionate power in determining the outcome of these deliberations. In this social interaction, choices need to be based on reasons which are, in principle, capable of being conveyed socially and adhering to some notion of impartiality, and not simply on self-interests, feelings, and opinions of individuals. Thus, functionings and capabilities can have a social dimension because social groups can have a shared understandings of what is valuable, although they can also be given an individualized interpretation in the sense that individuals can value them with good reason.

Some aspects of three types of social or collective goods may be briefly mentioned because of the attention they often receive. Regarding the environment, or different aspects of it, although it can be considered valuable because it provides utility for individuals, it is not clear how the utility of people who are not yet born can be taken into account, or how we can find out how many people will exist at some future date so that we can add their individual utility, or how we can know the complex and uncertain interactions that exist between economic activity and the environment and between different aspects of the environment. Because of these reasons, it would be sensible to proceed by measuring different aspects of environmental quality and treating improvements in them as representing development as an intrinsic good, if only in a provisional sense (because we do not know how they will affect us individually). Moreover, what goals we set ourselves regarding environmental quality requires shared values and understandings, and not everyone will be in agreement with them. Regarding freedoms and liberties, there needs to be a shared understanding of what kinds of freedoms require protection (such as, the freedom to live and work where one chooses without being prevented by other people or the state, the freedom to associate with others without interference, and the positive freedom to obtain health care and education), how the freedoms are defined, what to do in cases where different freedoms come into conflict, and how the freedoms are to be protected. Regarding rights, the same considerations apply. Moreover, the freedoms and rights have to apply to all in a society, unless there is good reason to restrict them in some cases. Rights and freedoms are also of interest because, unlike income and production, utility and the achievement of some functionings, which are concerned with consequences, they are deontological in nature and therefore focus on some aspects of development ignored by other approaches. However, they are difficult, if not impossible, to adequately quantify and aggregate, although there have been many attempts to do so.

One other thorny issue concerns to what extent a particular group of people within a country can define development in their own way and develop according to that definition when it is at odds with the definition shared by much of the rest of the country. This issue is particularly relevant for discussions on the rights and condition of many indigenous peoples around the world, such as the Scheduled Tribes and other Adivasis of India, who have often been viewed as standing in the way of 'development', interpreted as economic growth and the improvement of material conditions. A reasonable approach, which enables groups such as these to 'develop' using their own notion of 'development', raises several ethical and practical problems. Is it ethically acceptable for groups to deny some capabilities to some of their members, for instance, women? Should one leave these groups alone when they are located in areas rich in natural resources or particularly suitable for the construction of dams which could lead to improvements in the material conditions of large numbers of other people? Is it practical to expect that groups can pursue their own development goals when societies around them are following a different path and spreading the effects of that more broadly, for instance, through environmental damage and the spread of consumerism? The issue actually is a more general one, since the same questions arise regarding individuals or any groups within a given country, and for particular countries within a globalizing world. To take it further, it raises questions about whether widely accepted interpretations of the term 'development' can allow for the existence of alternative notions, an issue which is related to problems raised by the critics of development.

Evaluating Development

What does our discussion of different approaches to development imply about the questions raised earlier regarding the different dimensions of development? First, even though we may be most interested in the development of individual human beings, there are reasons why we can also focus on groups of people, animals, the inanimate, and conceptual systems. Second, there are strengths and shortcomings of all single metrics of development, such as income and production, utility, functionings, and capabilities. Thus, no single approach trumps the others and we need to take several of them into account. Third, although actual outcomes are important, we need to also take into account procedural aspects of development, examining rights and freedoms as well. Fourth, any notion of development needs to take into account the views of the people involved in the process, rather than having a few views of development thrust upon them by outside 'experts' or powerful groups. However, these views need to be based on reason and have a social character. Complex issues arise on how individuals and societies can arrive at some workable agreements about what development means or, at least, in the sense of what direction to go. Fifth, development encompasses many aspects of life, but there is something to be said for being somewhat narrow. We will narrow our focus in this book to *economic* development, rather than all possible aspects of development. Aside from being somewhat focused, this allows us to sidestep debates about political and social development related to democracy and governance (which are notoriously difficult to define and measure), and modernization (which apart, from definitional and measurement problems, leads to many controversies emphasized by post-development scholars). However, while we will focus on economic factors, we do so with some hesitation, since it is not clear how one can decide what is economic and what is not. Non-economic factors will not be banished entirely, because they may well be relevant for some concepts of development used by economists, such as utility (which can depend on non-economic issues such as the strength of community relations or the nature of political systems) and functionings and capabilities (which can depend on self-respect and dignity), and because they interact with these and other even narrower economic concepts like income and production. Finally, regarding means versus ends, we need to consider both. Many aspects of development can be seen as means as well as ends (for instance, improving education can be an end because it enhances functionings and capabilities, but can be a means to increasing income and production). Also, how one thinks of the so-called ends can and does change with time as new problems emerge (for instance, as reflected in the attention given to the natural environment in the last several decades). Moreover, an excessive focus on means can cloud our vision about what is truly important. For instance, while we should not equate economic development to economic growth in terms of per capita income and production because it neglects distributional and environmental issues, and ignores functionings and capabilities, rights and freedoms, and collective goods, we should not underestimate its importance. This is because it has proved very difficult to improve other aspects of development, such as functionings, in a sustained way without long-term increases in production and income and the distribution of income.

Given these answers, how do we evaluate development? Clearly, since economic development has many dimensions, no single indicator or narrow range of indicators will do. However, even for a particular concept of development, how do we assess whether a country or other unit is doing well in terms of it?

One approach is to interpret the level of achievement and improvement as evidence that the country is doing well and therefore developing. The level of achievement is hard to evaluate without a point of reference and an improvement is rather arbitrary, since it takes no improvement as the only point of comparison. An alternative approach is to examine how the unit is doing in comparison to some norm, such as, how it is doing compared to an earlier period, how it is doing compared to other comparable units, or how it is doing compared to its potential. Since it is difficult to ascertain the potential of a country or other unit—although imaginative methods can be and have been developed involving statistical and other methods—it may be easiest to use the other two norms, especially using other comparable periods and units, as a point of comparison.

To illustrate, we examine a few indicators. Table 1 presents data on per capita GDP, PPP-adjusted per capital GDP, the United Nations Development

Program's (UNDP's) HDI, and some health and education indicators. In terms of per capita income and production, LDCs such as India are far below more developed countries like Japan and the US, although the difference narrows somewhat in PPP terms because of lower prices of many goods and services.

India is also far below Brazil, Mexico, and China, but compares favourably to neighbours Bangladesh and Pakistan. These differences are also found in the HDI and health and education indicators. (Some countries, such as Brazil, have gross school enrolment rates over 100 per cent because some people who are not in the secondary school age population can be enrolled.) The table shows that although there is a positive relation between income and production measures and other indicators, it is possible for some countries to achieve high human development measures even with low income and production levels, due especially to successful public efforts. For instance, Cuba, with a considerably lower level of per capita GDP than Japan and the US, has high levels of functionings in terms of health and education indicators. Nigeria lags behind some other countries with comparable income and production measures in terms of health and education.

TABLE 1 Selected Production and Human Development Indicators, Selected Countries

	Per Capita GDP ($), 2011	Per Capita GDP ($), PPP 2011	Human Development Index, 2011	Life Expectancy at Birth (years), 2005–10	Infant Mortality Rate (per 1000 live births), 2005–10	Adult Literacy (%), 2011	Secondary School Enrolment (gross) (%), 2005–11
Bangladesh	743	1777	0.500	64.1	48.98	56	49
Brazil	12594	11640	0.718	72.4	23.47	90	101
China	5445	8400	0.687	73.0	21.99	96	81
Cuba	*5437	**9900	0.766	78.3	5.12	99	89
India	1489	3627	0.574	64.7	52.91	74	60
Japan	45903	34314	0.901	82.6	2.62	99	102
Mexico	10047	15266	0.770	76.2	16.66	93	87
Nigeria	1501	2533	0.459	46.9	96.14	67	44
Pakistan	1189	2745	0.504	. 65.5	70.90	58	34
Sri Lanka	2835	5581	0.691	72.4	12.44	94	87
USA	48112	48112	0.910	78.2	6.81	99	96
World Average	10035	11594	0.679	76.2	49.40	84	

Source: The World Bank, World DataBank, UNDP, *Human Development Report,* *2009 **2010 est., CIA World Factbook.

Bangladesh has done well in terms of infant mortality compared to India, but not in terms of education.

Figure 1 shows levels of per capita GDP in dollar values at constant prices for a few countries. The strong performance of South Korea is shown in the figure: Starting below Brazil and at a level not much higher than the other countries, Korea has experienced significant increases in per capita GDP. Since it is hard to see the curves for China, India, and Kenya, Figure 2 shows the logarithms of per capita GDP, indicating the differences more clearly. The curves in this figure also have the property that the slope of the curves shows the growth rate of per capita GDP. This figure shows China's strong growth performance since the mid-1970s, starting below all the other countries in the 1960s, overtaking India and Kenya and approach Brazil's per capita production level and narrowing the gap with South Korea. Brazil and Kenya show low growth performance, whereas India's growth rate has increased since the mid-1980s.

Table 2 presents data on poverty, inequality, and happiness measures for selected countries. The poverty rates use the same poverty level, although adjusting for

44

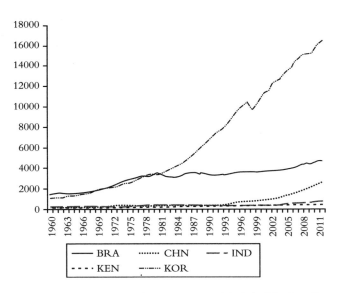

FIGURE 1   Per Capita GDP, Constant 2000 (US$): Brazil, China, India, Kenya, South Korea
Source: The World Bank, World DataBank.

PPP, and show, as one would expect, higher poverty rates for countries with lower per capita income and production levels. However, some low-income countries do well compared to some others. Sri Lanka fares better than its South Asian neighbours and Pakistan has

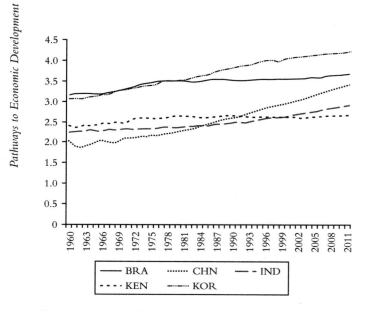

FIGURE 2   Log of Per Capita GDP, Constant 2000 (US$):
Brazil, China, India, Kenya, South Korea
Source: The World Bank, World DataBank.

lower poverty rates than does India. For reasons mentioned earlier, poverty rates are not necessarily good
measures of destitution and inequality measures may
be more enlightening. The Gini coefficient measures
shown in the figures are not strictly comparable across
countries, given different measurement methods; for

instance, some countries examine income and others consumer expenditures. However, the high levels of inequality in Brazil and South Africa stand out, as does that for the US among more developed countries. Although India's is low by the standards of the Latin American and African countries in the table, India's Gini coefficient has gone up from 30.8 in 1994 to 33.4 in 2005, and other evidence also points to increases in income inequality in India. As noted earlier, there are important dimensions to inequality other than vertical inequality in terms of income. The table shows inequality in terms of education with the ratio of the female literacy rate and the male literacy rate, with a lower number showing greater inequality. Pakistan is at the bottom of the list, followed by India, while Bangladesh is doing better. China, Kenya, Indonesia, and South Africa are doing better still, as are the Latin American countries which, of course, have significantly higher levels of per capita production and income. The table also shows happiness indicators as a measure of utility from the most recent year in which survey results are reported in the World Values Survey. Among the countries shown, India has the lowest level of subjective well-being, although those of Bangladesh and Pakistan are

TABLE 2 Selected Poverty, Inequality, and Happiness Indicators, Selected Countries

	Poverty Rate ($2 a day PPP), 2005–10	Poverty Rate ($1.25 a day PPP), 2005–10	Gini Coefficient 2002–10	Literacy Rate (Female to Male Ratio), 2007–10	Happiness Index* 2001–8
Bangladesh	76.54	43.25	32.1	0.85	154.9
Brazil	10.82	6.14	54.7	1.00	172.3
China	29.79	13.06	42.5	0.95	153.1
India	68.72	32.67	33.4	0.68	151.0
Indonesia	46.12	18.06	34.0	0.94	185.7
Japan			38.1		177.2
Kenya	67.21	43.37	47.7	0.93	
Korea, South			31.3		174.8
Mexico	5.19	1.15	48.3	0.97	158.8
Nigeria	84.49	67.98	48.8	0.70	183.7
Pakistan	60.19	21.04	30.0	0.59	152.5
South Africa	31.33	13.77	63.1	0.96	156.0
Sri Lanka	29.13	7.04	40.3	0.97	
UK			34.0		187.0
USA			45.0		186.3

Sources: The World Bank, World Database, ★ World Values Survey.

comparable. Some LDCs, such as Indonesia and Nigeria, are doing well in terms of this measure, better than Japan and close to the UK and the USA. More developed countries are seen to be doing better in the table, but among all such countries, there is no clear relationship between income and happiness.

Finally, Table 3 shows some environmental indicators. Freshwater withdrawals reflect geographical features, but also provide some indication of water shortage. India and, especially, Pakistan are seen to have a problem on this score. CO_2 emissions are a measure of air pollution and also show a country's contribution to global climate change. In per capita terms, the figures show that more developed countries like Japan, the UK, and, especially, the USA, are the major sources of emission, although South Africa and China are also major polluters. However, as a ratio of production, LDCs have high levels of emissions which imply problems for air quality as their income and production increase unless they are able to reduce the pollution-intensity of production, for instance, by switching to technology that is less pollution-intensive, or a product mix that is less polluting.

TABLE 3 Selected Environmental Indicators, Selected Countries

	Annual Freshwater Withdrawals (% of Internal Resources), 2011	CO_2 Emissions (Metric Tons Per Capita), 2009	CO_2 Emissions (kg per PPP $ of GDP), 2009
Bangladesh	34.1619	0.347121	0.222394
Brazil	1.071798	1.89989	0.18242
China	19.69783	5.773794	0.845768
India	52.62794	1.638949	0.529762
Indonesia	5.611689	1.902924	0.468031
Japan	20.93953	8.632422	0.269356
Kenya	13.21256	0.312969	0.197327
Korea, South	39.27525	10.35695	0.385284
Mexico	19.511	3.983074	0.289899
Nigeria	4.665158	0.454624	0.203661
Pakistan	333.6364	0.945601	0.364729
South Africa	27.90179	10.1179	0.983176
Sri Lanka	24.52652	0.618997	0.130818
UK	8.958621	7.67791	0.223285
USA	16.97658	17.27528	0.38131

Source: The World Bank, World Database.

3

Domestic Economic Aspects
of Development

To gain insights into how LDCs can develop, we need
to understand what prevents development. Economists
and other social scientists have identified a variety
of obstacles to development, the major ones among
which we discuss in this and the following two chapters. In this chapter, we discuss those domestic factors
that have been traditionally emphasized by economists,
which can be called 'economic'. In the next chapter,
we will examine international factors, continuing to
focus on economic factors, and in the following one we
will examine those that have been emphasized mostly
by other social scientists, so that we call them 'non-
economic' (although recognizing that the boundary
between them and the economic factors is blurred).

Vicious Cycles of Poverty

A fruitful starting point for analysing obstacles to development is the concept of the vicious cycle of poverty, which states that poor countries stay poor because they *are* poor (where the word poor is used broadly to refer to the less developed in a variety of senses). Although the idea is simple and appealing, it raises a number of questions and issues.

First, the concept is not very useful unless we can come up with specific mechanisms which make poor countries stay poor. Development scholars have suggested a number of mechanisms—such as low levels of saving and poor health conditions—which can explain the vicious cycle of the form: poverty implies some conditions which imply its persistence. Thus, poverty, in the sense of low levels of income, implies that people cannot save to add to their wealth or invest to increase future production and income because they devote all their income towards meeting subsistence needs. Poverty, in the sense of having low levels of education, implies that people have low levels of income, which then makes it difficult for them to afford education for themselves and their children. Much of the rest of this

52

and the two following chapters can be interpreted as spelling out some of these mechanisms in more detail.

Second, the approach needs to go beyond just saying that poverty creates the conditions which reinforce it, because it is possible that if some small steps can be taken to reduce poverty, the conditions for its existence will weaken, and a cumulative development process will be set in motion. What appears initially to be a vicious cycle can turn out to be a virtuous one. Two cases can be contrasted, as shown in Figure 3. The figure shows the relationship between the level of some development variable, y, which we can, for the sake of concreteness, take as income or health conditions, and the changes in it over time, which we denote by $\dot{y}$ (with the dot over

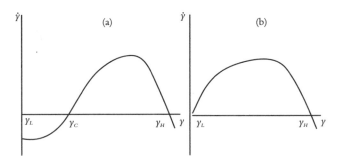

FIGURE 3 Vicious and Virtuous Cycles of Poverty

the variable denoting changes over time). When $\dot{y}$ is positive, y increases over time, while when $\dot{y}$ is negative y falls over time. Both cases show that when y increases $\dot{y}$ first increases and then decreases, eventually becoming negative, after the level shown as y_H. The negatively-sloped segment may exist because at least for some indicators of development (such as, say, life expectancy), perpetual increases are not possible. However, for other indicators there may be no negatively sloped segment; for instance, income can increase indefinitely. Whether or not the curve eventually has a negative slope and crosses the horizontal axis is not important for our purposes. What is crucial is what happens at lower levels of y.

In case (a), the relation is such that at low levels of y, $\dot{y}$ is negative. Thus, when y increases, although its decline becomes smaller or its rise larger (since the relation between y and $\dot{y}$ is positive), y falls over time. This can happen, for instance, because at low levels of output farm families eat a large part of their crop to meet their subsistence needs, not sowing enough to increase their output in the next year, making production fall over time. It is only when production increases beyond a certain level, y_C (where the subscript C denotes critical level), that farmers are able to sow more than the previous year, and output begins to increase, so that $\dot{y}$ is positive. If the individual, family, or the economy as a whole, starts with a low level of y, say y_L (which is zero in the figure, but can also be a very low amount), and some change makes their output rise to a level less than y_C, y will fall over time back to y_L. However, if somehow y is pushed beyond y_C, it will rise over time and reach the high level y_H (or continue to increase indefinitely if the curve does not eventually cross the horizontal axis). In case (b), the relationship is such that if y increases by even a little above y_L, it will continue increasing till it reaches y_H (or increase continually). In case (a), it is reasonable to think of the economy being trapped at a vicious cycle at y_L, whereas in case (b), any upward movement from y_L results in a vicious cycle upwards. The crucial issue for the idea of the vicious cycle is whether increases in y lead to $\dot{y}$ becoming negative or positive. The existence of a vicious cycle requires that the relationship resembles case (a) rather than case (b). If a vicious cycle exists, development is difficult because considerable effort may be required to push the economy beyond y_C; otherwise the economy reverts back to its low-level trap.

Third, since different development variables—such as health and education indicators—may be causally related, for instance, bad health prevents children from going to school, and poor education results in unhygienic practices, it is sometimes not sensible to think of the dynamics of a single indicator in isolation. Several implications follow from this observation. One, a vicious cycle for, or involving, one indicator may block overall development even in the absence of a vicious cycle for another one considered in isolation. For instance, if the dynamics of health is like case (a) above—considered in isolation, for a given level of education—while that of education is like case (b), also for a given level of health, the overall dynamics can exhibit a vicious cycle. Two, if there are several interacting vicious cycles, the effort required in breaking out of the resulting vicious cycle may be very high since effort is required on both health and education fronts.

Fourth, we have not specified at what level (for instance, micro or macro) the cycles apply. In general, obstacles to development can arise at different levels: at the level of individuals or families or small groups, what is called the micro level; at the level of the economy

as a whole, called the macro level; at some intermediate level of broad sectors or large groups; or at the
world or global level. Micro-level obstacles can be
analysed without necessarily referring to the broader
economy or society in which they operate, but can
also sometimes be used to examine overall problems
with the economy and society since, for some issues
and some situations, the whole behaves like the sum of
its parts. However, there are many obstacles that require
analysing interactions between different individuals or
small groups, or how individual behaviour affects, and
is in turn affected by, sectoral or macro conditions,
which requires us to go beyond the micro level. For
instance, in a famous example discussed by Rosenstein-
Rodan (1943), individual firms, in contemplating
increases in their production, may not expect to find
buyers and sell enough to be able to warrant the expansion, and are therefore discouraged from expanding
production. However, if a large number of firms which
produce different products expand production more or
less simultaneously, the employment and income that
they generate can create the demand for each other.
Thus, a sufficiently large increase in total production
spread over many firms, perhaps with government

spending, can generate enough demand to make further increases in output profitable. Cycles can also appear due to the interaction of different broad sectors which can only be analysed at the systemic level. For instance, the interaction between an agricultural sector with surplus labour and a manufacturing sector with increasing returns to scale (to be discussed later in this chapter when we consider sectoral issues) can lead to vicious cycles which require a large expansion of the manufacturing sector to reap sufficient advantages of large scale production (Ros 2001). It should be noted that although analysis at the sectoral or macro level is crucial for understanding many obstacles to development, it can be misleading or incomplete if it does not take into account how individual people or groups behave. Finally, some issues, such as global climate change, require analysis at the global level, although how countries are affected by them may depend on factors internal to them.

Fifth, although the curves show a simple relation between y and $\dot{y}$, it should be recognized that they actually incorporate a number of different causal mechanisms influenced by behavioural relations involving choices people make (which can be at least partially affected by social norms), the objective circumstances in which people find themselves and their expectations about the future. For instance, in the cycle in which income determines education and therefore a change in income, the level of income can affect whether or not people send their children to school through a number of different channels, including whether people can afford to send them to school (in terms of schooling and other related fees and whether they need their children to work instead of going to school), the availability of schools close by (which depends on average income which in turn affects government revenues), people's expectations regarding whether their children's income will increase as a result of obtaining education, and on whether the increase in education actually increases income in the future due to the availability of suitable jobs. These observations imply that it may be possible to break out of vicious cycles in some cases by shifting the curves by affecting their underlying relationships, thereby reducing the level of y_C, rather than by requiring a large increase in y to go beyond y_C.

Finally, to go from general ideas about vicious and virtuous cycles to specific mechanisms, we can start by examining the process of production, taking into account the fact that people receive income from the production of goods and services which use resources, inputs, or factors of production. The factors of production economists focus on are labour and capital. More workers, by expending more labour, can produce more output, as can better workers, for instance, those who are more skilled. Capital is interpreted either as financial resources used to obtain the means of production or the physical means of production themselves, that is, machinery, equipment, factory buildings, and infrastructure such as transport and communication systems. With more and better machines and other capital, it is likely that a given number of people can produce more: consider farmers who install pump-sets and tractors to increase agricultural production. There are, of course, other inputs, such as natural resources and land, which are particularly important in the production of agricultural goods and produced inputs. To study the relationship between income and production (an example of the level of y) and their increases over time (an example of $\dot{y}$), we can examine how given initial levels of income and production make possible the expansion of income and production due to increases in capital, in the quantity and quality of labour and other inputs, and changes in how productively these inputs are used in production.

Saving, Investment, and Capital Formation

We start with the accumulation of capital, long stressed by economists. Many of them, including Adam Smith, David Ricardo, and Karl Marx, in stressing the importance of capital accumulation in the growth process, focused on the importance of saving. Consider, for instance, farmers and other producers who receive income by selling some of their output. They can use this income for consumption purposes or save some of it to buy capital goods and increase their ability to produce more in the future. Early development economists emphasized the role of saving, pointing out that in LDCs poor people with low levels of production and income (partly due to low levels of capital) are unable to save much, having to devote most or all of their income to meeting subsistence consumption needs, and therefore cannot increase production over time. What is true of individuals is true for the LDC as a whole. Increases in income are devoted to meeting previously unmet basic consumption needs rather than to increasing saving, creating a vicious cycle.

While the story of the poor farmer's inability to save arguably applies to many poor people, it is not a very plausible explanation for low rates of capital accumulation and growth in many LDCs. We find that even people with very low levels of income in LDCs spend on social and religious ceremonies and consumer durables, sometimes skimping on basic subsistence needs such as nutritional food and proper health care, and saving very little. Even people who are capable of saving—all over the world—often do not do so because they seek immediate gratification rather than providing for the distant future and because of social norms and pressures to maintain status and social standing through consumption. These tendencies are arguably exacerbated in LDCs because of lower access to banks and voluntary employee saving accounts, and the powerful influence of cultural norms (for instance, for religious and marriage ceremonies). Moreover, not everyone in the LDCs is poor—with some receiving incomes high even by global standards—and organizations such as private firms and the government may also save, so that the argument does not apply to countries as a whole. Indeed, for 2009, saving as a ratio of GDP in many poor countries was higher (for instance, 54 per cent in China and 34 per cent for India) than in many rich countries (for instance, less than 11 per cent for the US and 23 per cent for Germany), which can be partly explained by the insecure conditions of lower-income people who seek some financial security through saving. High saving rates in low-income countries often result from high growth rates in income—since consumption increases do not, at least, initially rise as much as income rises because consumption partly depends on habits—so that high saving rates are likely to be the result of, rather than the cause of, high growth rates. Of course, even when people and organizations like private firms save, this does not automatically lead to investment, that is, the act of adding to productive capital, which requires sufficient incentives in the form of expected future profits. And even if some people and organizations do not save, they can invest by obtaining financing from others: for instance, poor street vendors may be able to borrow to buy carts for carrying their merchandise. Finally, even if investment does occur, the machines and equipment may not result in significant expansion in levels of output because of inefficiencies and excess capacity.

If the cause of low growth lies in a low rate of capital accumulation due to low saving, the solution to the problem can be found in encouraging people, including the poor, to save more, for instance, by making saving institutions more widely available, by providing greater incentives to save (such as higher interest rates), by channeling income to people and sectors that save more, and through government saving (that is, by increasing government revenues while keeping government spending low). Such efforts will allow individuals, including the poor, to increase their future income, and allow the economy as a whole to save and invest more and experience a higher rate of economic growth.

However, what if low capital accumulation is due to insufficient incentives for investment? Some early development economists, such as Nurkse (1967), argued that in addition to the vicious cycle of savings there is a vicious cycle of investment: firms in LDCs do not have sufficient incentives for investment because low levels of income prevent people from buying much, keeping the demand for goods and services low. Moreover, business firms in LDCs are exposed to problems such the vagaries of weather and political and social instability (and if we consider external factors, shocks due to changes in the price of their exports and international capital flows), which make future prospects uncertain. Low and uncertain profit expectations keep investment at low levels, whether from their own saving or from borrowed resources. In this situation, people may consume their incomes instead of saving and investing, implying a low rate of capital accumulation. It is worse still if, rather than spend their income on consumption, people save and hold on to money or buy assets such as gold, land, and shares (which can cause asset bubbles without promoting business investment), or even send their money abroad. The result is a low level of aggregate demand (for consumption and investment purposes) which reduces output and employment along the lines emphasized by John Maynard Keynes (1936) in his discussion of unemployment in advanced capitalist countries. Although such aggregate demand problems were not considered relevant for LDCs in the early days of development economics when saving and other supply-side constraints were stressed, it is now widely recognized that aggregate demand deficiency can reduce output and its growth in many, especially semi-industrialized, LDCs, partly due to the fragmented nature of goods and financial markets and partly due to the many and complex sources of uncertainty pervading these economies (Dutt 2013). Under these conditions, efforts to increase saving—by people (especially by increasing interest rates and the cost of capital) or by the government (by reducing government expenditure)—can paradoxically reduce saving and investment (which has been found to depend positively on output) by reducing aggregate demand, output, and income.

Investment can also be low because of the lack of financing. Many economists have been concerned with the problems that exist in LDCs because of the high levels of uncertainty which make lenders unwilling to lend (just as they make firms unwilling to invest) for fear of default by borrowers, especially to the poor with few assets, and hence, collateral, to offer. The only source of loans for many potential investors is the informal market, such as from moneylenders who charge very high interest rates, thereby reducing the incentive to invest. For the poor, microcredit organizations have found that it is feasible to lend to groups of the poor, especially women, who have low rates of default because they monitor the behaviour of other members of their group. Organizations such as the Grameen Bank, founded by Mohammed Yunus in Bangladesh, and the National Bank for Agriculture and Rural Development which lends to banks which in turn provide microcredit in India, have proliferated in many LDCs. Despite low default rates, however, it is unclear how effective such practices have been in increasing investment by, and raising income for, the poor. The overall flow of finance to potential investors can be expanded by encouraging the development of banks and other organizations, and markets in bonds and stocks, as well as by establishing government banks. However, financial markets in which private individuals and organizations operate in search of financial returns have occasionally exhibited a high degree of instability in rich countries and especially in LDCs: in boom times optimism about the future leads to large increases in borrowing and lending, often to finance the purchase of speculative assets which create asset bubbles rather than for productive investment, and this euphoria gives way to financial crashes, which then leads to pessimism and contraction. It is argued that this volatility can be controlled only with careful government regulation, which may be beyond the power of regulators in LDCs. Other economists and policymakers blame the problems of financial markets on government over-regulation, which keeps interest rates low, discouraging saving and the flow of the funds which enter financial markets, and prevents the allocation of finance to the most profitable uses to promote investment and growth.

Population, Education, and Health

While the greater availability of capital is likely to result in increases in total as well as per capita production and income, this is not necessarily the case when the number of people in the economy increases, for instance, due to population growth. Even if an increase in population increases the quantity of labour and this leads to an increase in total production, it does not necessarily follow that production and income per person also increases. Increases in population can change the age distribution of the population, for instance, increasing the proportion of children in the population and decreasing that of the working population, which results in a fall in income and production per person. It has also been observed that in many LDCs there is surplus labour in the sense that significant number of potential workers are unemployed or underemployed (due to the lack of sufficient amounts of capital and other inputs or the lack of aggregate demand), so that further increases in the number of workers merely increases the amount of labour surplus rather than increasing total output.

At low levels of income, people tend to have more children and larger families, implying that poor countries tend to experience high rates of population growth (unless they are too poor to allow enough people to survive). Faster population growth can occur because people find it advantageous to have more children, to ensure that some of them will care for them in old age (since poor countries usually do not have government-sponsored services to care for them) and because with low levels of education and the lack of employment opportunities, women, who bear much of the burden of childbirth and childrearing, have a smaller say in decisions regarding whether or not to have children.

Larger families and faster population growth, in turn, dilutes the resources available to families and keeps them in poverty, strains the economy as a whole, reducing its ability to adequately feed, house, employ, provide health care for, and educate the larger numbers, and ultimately strains the natural environment. It is sometimes argued that population pressures can stimulate technological change (as has sometimes been observed in agricultural regions which switch to more productive methods) and larger populations imply a larger number of inventive geniuses (assuming that geniuses comprise a constant fraction of the population), but these effects are unlikely in situations where population growth is very rapid, population density is already high, and where educational and job opportunities are scarce.

The combination of high and increasing population growth rates and the dilution of resources by growing populations means that a significant increase in income may be required for population growth to fall sufficiently as people become less poor and begin to see the advantages of smaller families. Some LDCs, including India, have experienced a reduction in overall population growth rates as a result of what is called the demographic transition. However, many others, including several in Africa, experience high population growth, as do some states in India, such as Bihar.

Poor countries and people also have inadequate resources to put into improving the availability and quality of education, which results in low levels of functionings and capabilities related to education. Even when governments are able to set up schools, families may have little incentive to keep children in schools when they believe—whether such beliefs are warranted or not—that children will not be able to obtain higher incomes by attending school, and can instead do more for their families by working. Low levels of education, in turn, keep incomes of people low since they are unable to obtain better paying jobs. For the country as a whole, low levels of education can slow down technological change and constrain the expansion of production due to shortages of labour with appropriate skills; statistical evidence suggests that countries which accumulate more 'human capital' as measured by, say, average years of schooling, tend to experience—other things constant—higher rates of growth.

Poor health also reduces the ability of people to work effectively and reduces labour productivity, reducing income, and low levels of income lead to poor health due to low levels of nutrition and inadequate resources for preventative health care. The state in countries with low levels of income cannot raise enough revenues to fund adequate health services that can be effective in improving public health. Poor health conditions reduce the functionings and capabilities of people by reducing the length of their lives (even resulting in the death of large numbers of infants and children) and increases human suffering due to illness and disability.

Low levels of functionings in terms of education and health can perpetuate problems for each. Low levels of education among parents can lead to poor choices regarding education and inadequate home support for it (although there are many poor people who go to extraordinary lengths to educate their children), while poor health, especially of pregnant women, may have adverse consequences for the health of children. Moreover, as mentioned earlier, low levels of education and health also adversely affect improvements in each other. Low levels of education lead to inadequate knowledge about health matters, while poor health prevents school attendance and adversely affects education.

There are many obvious policies which can be adopted to reduce these problems. Tough policies of imposing penalties on large families by withdrawing resources from them (as done in China) and sterilization campaigns (as in India in the past), aside from violating some individual rights, have been known to have undesirable consequences, such as the selective abortion or neglect (and worse) of females, and the use of coercion by government officials. In any case, less drastic measures, such as the education and empowerment of women with the provision of resources for birth control, and improvements in income and resources of the poor, are less coercive and more effective in reducing population growth. The need for increasing government resources to education and health is obvious, but fulfilling these needs is often neglected because of other items, which often get priority, such as military expenditure and subsidies to the politically powerful. Even if resources are available, regions and people who are the least politically powerful and who need them the most may not be able to effectively demand and have access to health and education facilities; or the quality of services provided—due to teacher and health worker absenteeism, for instance—may be poor.

Even when the resources are available, people may not use them because of behavioural inertia (which is not confined to the poor but even afflict the well-off in rich countries) and because of the lack of incentives (in the absence of job prospects). Raising productivity by improving education and health conditions may not even increase income if there is an overall lack of capital and effective demand and, instead, increase unemployment or underemployment.

Efficiency and Technology

Many economists criticize the overemphasis on resources, especially capital, and focus more on how these resources are used, that is, their level of productivity and the rate of productivity growth.

Low levels of productivity of resources (beyond what is due to the low quality of these resources, for instance, because of poor education and health) can be caused by a variety of factors. They can be due to the absence of incentives for people and organizations to produce as much as they can (for instance, due to the lack of demand), the lack of other resources required for production such as electricity and imported raw materials (because of shortages in power supply or foreign exchange), and because of laziness or avoidable mistakes. These problems are usually not emphasized by mainstream economists, who typically assume that people and organizations are self-interested maximizers (in the sense of achieving their highest levels of income, profits, or utility), that they can substitute between different inputs, and because prices adjust to increase demand. Some analysts do take into account the fact that individuals and organizations may not actually be 'rational' maximizers (if any precise meaning can be attached to that term): for instance, in some situations with insufficient competition, they do not exert much effort, sometimes they simply do not have enough information to make appropriate decisions, and the actions of organizations may reflect the interests and power of different people and groups who comprise them in ways that are not in the best for the organization as a whole.

Rather than focusing on productive efficiency, that is, the efficiency of resources in a given use, mainstream economists stress what is called allocative efficiency, that is, the allocation of resources between alternative uses (that is, the production of different goods and by different firms) in a way that maximizes the value of total production. The analysis is conducted using standard neoclassical economic theory, which sees economic agents and firms as 'rational' maximizers who pursue their self-interest, operating in smoothly functioning markets. Efficiency is defined in terms of the notion of Pareto optimality, which states that a situation is efficient if it is not possible to make any individual better off (in terms of his or her own reckoning) without making someone else worse off; in other words, there are no opportunities to make costless improvements in people's well-being. The efficiency of free market outcomes is demonstrated using the so-called fundamental theorem of welfare economics which states that if all markets are perfectly competitive, under certain conditions (to be mentioned later), the free market outcome is efficient in the sense of being Pareto optimal. Perfect competition refers to situations in which, among other things, markets have many buyers and sellers, so that none of them can individually control prices, which are instead determined by impersonal forces of market demand and supply. Basically, free markets lead to the optimal allocation of resources: if there is a shortage in some markets, the price will rise in that market, and conversely if there is an oversupply. Suppliers, observing higher prices, have an incentive to produce more, while less will be produced in markets with lower prices, and consumers also receive signals to buy more of cheaper products where there is an oversupply. Thus, the price mechanism shifts resources across sectors to achieve allocative efficiency.

Some mainstream economists assume that actual economies come close to the conditions required for the welfare theorem to hold, and therefore argue that in fact the obstacles to development are created by government restrictions and controls—for instance, taxes and subsidies, price controls, and the government ownership of enterprises—which interfere with the free operation of markets. However, other economists—including many who follow the mainstream approach—argue that the assumptions of the theorem are, in fact, not satisfied in actual economies, especially in LDCs. Some examples of violations of the conditions include the following. First, there are departures from perfect competition which cause inefficiency; for instance, monopolistic or oligopolistic producers (that is, markets with one or a few sellers) may produce less than what is efficient for the economy because they restrict their production levels in order to keep up the price of their product and, hence, profits high. Second, there are externalities in the sense that people and firms affect others adversely or positively without either paying or being paid. For instance, firms may emit too much pollution which makes other firms and people worse off because the latter—rather than they—bear the costs of pollution. There may be imperfect information, in the sense that buyers and sellers do not possess all the relevant information to make decisions which lead to efficient outcomes. For instance, lenders may not have information about what borrowers do after they borrow (that is, whether or not they devote the time and attention to engage in profitable activity so that they can pay back the loans rather than default), and thus, may not be willing to lend to them and thereby allow them to increase production and profits and receive interest payments. Going beyond the standard mainstream approach, if one takes the future to be uncertain (in the sense discussed by Keynes), so that it cannot be predicted in objectively probabilistic terms, people and firms may often not have the confidence to increase production, investment, and lending, and many mutually beneficial exchanges and activities will not occur. Finally, there are public goods, such as transport and communication services, for many of which it is difficult to exclude those who do not pay but use them, and which can be used by many at the same time without compromising the ability of others of using them, and which, therefore, will not be produced in efficient amounts by private producers. If such market failures exist in LDCs, and especially if they are quite commonplace, then having free markets without much government interference will not necessarily result in efficiency. Many obstacles to development may be explained in terms of such market failures. For instance, the presence of the free rider problem and the prevalence of positive externalities imply that private individuals and organizations will not undertake many activities which can promote growth and reduce poverty.

It may be sensible to focus on increasing productivity over time, and indeed some have questioned whether it is useful to distinguish between attempting to become more productive now and attempting to increase the growth of productivity over time. Such as increase in productivity is associated with improvements in technology, that is, technical methods by which inputs are used to produce outputs, but also by changes in other factors such as norms regarding the pace of work and the cooperation between different groups and individuals involved in the production process. Although the determinants of technological change are complex, it can be argued that its rate depends on the amount of research and development activity, the quantity and quality of education, and the experience that producers gain by producing and investing. LDCs may be caught in vicious cycles because they do not typically have the resources to invest significantly in research and development and education, and they lack incentives to increase output and investment because of small and slow-growing markets and other factors. Changes in work norms and industrial relations are also likely to be adversely affected by low wages, implying that workers have fewer incentives to increase their productivity and cooperate with employers.

Poverty and Inequality

So far we have focused mainly on income, production, and growth due to increases in the amounts of resources and the efficiency with which these resources are used. Other aspects of development, such as functionings and capabilities, were only briefly mentioned. But development also refers to other things, such as poverty, inequality, and the environment.

As discussed in the previous chapter, poverty and inequality (in income and in other indicators such as health and education) can be considered to be intrinsic aspects of development. In addition, poverty and inequality are related to other aspects of development. Obviously, high levels of income poverty imply low levels of health and education among the poor. Less obviously, poverty and inequality can affect economic growth. A fair amount of empirical work suggests that countries with lower levels of income poverty and inequality tend to experience higher rates of income growth and various plausible mechanisms to explain this have been proposed (The World Bank 2005). Higher incomes for the poor and lower levels of income inequality, which imply a lower income share of the rich with a higher saving rate and a higher one for the poor who consume most of their income, increases the market for goods and output and the utilization of capacity in countries in which growth is determined by aggregate demand, and this can increase investment incentives and the rate of capital accumulation and

81

growth. This will not happen, however, in countries in which growth is determined by saving and which do not face aggregate demand problems, where more income equality can actually reduce saving, and hence investment and growth. High levels of inequality and poverty also imply low levels of health and education for many people, resulting in low levels of productivity and its growth. Moreover, because of the absence or low levels of assets, the poor do not get access to credit and the ability to increase their income through productive activities which require financing; thus, high levels of poverty reduce the overall rate of growth of the economy. Finally, high levels of inequality can lead to lower levels of productivity in activities which require greater cooperation and trust between people with different income levels and results in political unrest and redistribution with possible adverse consequences, which can reduce levels of output and growth. However, for activities of relatively smaller groups where benefits from the activity accrue to everyone whether they contribute or not—such as village irrigation projects—high inequality levels may overcome what is called the free-rider problem (in which no one contributes because they want a free-ride on the contributions of others) by giving the rich the incentive to get things done since they are the major beneficiaries of such activities; in such cases inequality can promote higher output levels and growth.

LDCs have high levels of poverty and often have high levels of inequality. Obviously, low per capita income, given the distribution of income over income groups, implies a high incidence of income poverty, and higher inequality in income given average income levels is also associated more with income poverty. Higher income countries are typically associated with lower levels of absolute income poverty, and increases in income are typically, though not invariably, associated with decreases in the income poverty. The problem is that income inequality can increase with increases in average incomes. The Kuznets curve, named after Simon Kuznets, who examined the relationship using empirical data, suggests that as average income increases (comparing different countries or within a country over time), income inequality first tends to rise and then fall. Explanations of this relation rely on sectoral shifts in income and employment—for instance, shifts from peasant agriculture where most people have low incomes to capitalist manufacturing in which wages are initially low and profit high, and then to services in which especially high skilled workers can get high wages; the spread of education initially confined to a few and then broadening, rising wages due to increases in the demand for labour brought about by the expansion in output and the diminution of the subsistence economy, a sector which provides a source of cheap labour, and ameliorative and redistributive government policies, especially in so-called welfare states. The curve provides an optimistic picture for those who value equality; even though it gets worse in terms of inequality when an economy experiences income growth, subsequently it will get better. However, the Kuznets story does not hold everywhere and a little reflection on the nature of the relationship between average income and income inequality makes it clear why this is so. The relationship is affected by the speed and direction of technological change: rapid technological change which increases the productivity of labour may slow down employment growth and exert downward pressure on wages, and what is called skill-biased technological change can increase the ratio of the wages of high-skilled to low-skilled workers. It also depends on the degree of openness of the education system (including the availability of student loans and grants), the distribution of assets (especially in poor, agrarian economies), and the nature of government expenditure and taxation policies, among other determinants.

Inequality can exist not only in the form of inequality of income between the rich and the poor (an example of what is called vertical inequality), but also inequality of income and other indicators of functionings and capabilities between different groups of people, such as different ethnic groups, people living in different parts of the country, and between men and women (which is referred to as horizontal inequality). Consider gender inequality, a problem that is reflected in their significantly lower income, asset ownership, and functionings, for instance, in terms of nutrition and education, of women in most LDCs and indeed even in higher infant and child mortality among girls (due to neglect and worse conditions). The problem emerges not only from the uneven balance of power within the family but is also reflected in social norms and legal institutions and the distribution of political power among men and women. This is a major problem for about a half of humanity and, additionally, results in problems for development in general, for instance, by resulting in high population growth rates and adversely affecting the education and health of children.

Policies to reduce poverty include cash transfer programmes to the poor (which also attempt to address other related problems by imposing conditions, such as the school enrolment of children), improvements in the availability of education, health, and food for the poor, employment guarantee schemes which pay low wages to provide employment to those who cannot find employment at a higher wage (like India's rural employment guarantee scheme), and providing micro-credit to the poor (which often provides group loans to the poor, especially women). Inequality can be addressed by these measures, making education more accessible to lower income groups, by transferring income through government fiscal policy, by transferring assets, for instance, land through land reforms, and through affirmative action and other preferential policies for disadvantaged groups. Poverty and inequality can also be reduced by making economic growth more inclusive, for instance, by ensuring that output growth occurs in sectors where its effect on employment growth is high.

The Environment

The natural environment has various dimensions, such as clean air and water, land quality, forests, animal stocks and biodiversity, weather conditions, and global climate. As mentioned in the previous chapter, we can take improvements in environmental quality to be an intrinsic aspect of development, so that environment degradation can be seen directly as a development problem. Moreover, environmental damage can adversely affect other aspects of development. The lack of suitable supplies of water and the loss of soil nutrients and soil erosion has a negative effect on agricultural productivity, damage to common property resources can affect an important source of livelihood in LDCs, pollutants in the air and water cause major health hazards and reduce life expectancy, and a high level of pollution requires resources to be devoted to amelioration, adversely affecting the amount of resources that can be devoted to capital accumulation and growth. Such problems are likely to affect the poor most adversely and worsen inequality because the poor are particularly vulnerable to the problem (since they are more likely to draw on common property resources for food and fuel and live in areas more susceptible to environmental damage) and least able to cope with it (for instance, with medical treatment), in turn due to their low levels of income.

Environmental problems exist all around the world, but are more severe in LDCs. Environmental degradation is often attributed to the problem of externalities: self-interested individuals damage the environment (by polluting, for instance) because, while it takes effort on their part not to do so, their actions do not hurt themselves much. However, the damage done by each, when aggregated, affects the overall environment and hurts them all. Government intervention in the form of effluent fees and other regulations are required to reduce the damage done, but this requires the will and the ability to enact and enforce laws. People and governments in LDCs have more immediate concerns in providing for basic consumption needs and seem to be less concerned about environmental problems in the future, and are less able to enforce environmental regulations. Moreover, even when individuals use their own land, they may overuse it and damage its quality to meet subsistence needs, and the absence of suitable infrastructure and income earning opportunities may make people in LDCs, especially the poor, pollute and stress common property environmental resources more than in rich countries. Finally, it has been argued that weaker property rights leads to more environmental damage, an issue we will take up in more detail in Chapter 5.

These considerations suggest that as LDCs experience increases in average incomes, they will experience less environmental damage. However, increases in production and consumption also tend to exacerbate environmental damage due to pollution caused by production (for instance, the emission of pollutants in the air, which can even lead to global warming due to the accumulation of greenhouse gases) and the use of natural resources for production and consumption (such as cutting trees and the depletion of nutrients in the soil). Some studies have found an inverse U-shaped relation between some measures of environmental damage (such as the stock of pollutants in the air or the flow effluents released) and per capita income, and by analogy with the income–inequality relation mentioned earlier, the relation has been called the environmental Kuznets curve (EKC). It suggests that while, at first, income growth results in more environmental damage, eventually, conditions improve, as countries get richer because they are more willing and able to contain the damage through regulations, better enforcement, and the development of cleaner and less resource-intensive technology. The optimism implicit in the EKC may not be justified, however. First, some indicators of environmental damage, such as carbon dioxide emissions, do not exhibit a negatively sloped segment. Second, the downward-sloping segment may in part be explained by shifts in the production of 'dirty' goods to LDCs. Third, many LDCs may have a long road ahead of them before they reach that segment. Finally, there may be pressures from different groups in society to make light of the problem (since it can reduce profits and consumption) as seems to have happened in some rich countries.

Standard methods of reducing environmental damage, by overcoming problems due to externalities, involve using pollution taxes, restricting pollution with quantitative standards, and creating markets using tradable permits, which allow holders of permits to pollute (and inducing those potential polluters who can reduce their pollution, for instance, by adopting less polluting technology) to reduce pollution to a desired level. To the extent that environmental damage is due to the tragedy of the commons, the privatization of common property resources has sometimes been recommended. However, this overlooks the informal and customary solutions some communities have developed that maintain their common property resources which are used by them (Ostrom 1990). Moreover, some environmental problems, which are the result of poverty (such as the overuse of private land and the commons for the sake of survival), the lack of infrastructure (such as sanitation), and information about the effects of certain activities (such as the production of excessive solid waste), require policies to reduce poverty and improve infrastructure, and, generally, to raise public awareness regarding the problem.

Sectoral Constraints

While we have so far examined overall obstacles to development, sometimes obstacles which afflict particular sectors of the economy can have a negative effect on the economy as a whole. For such obstacles we need to understand how the development of particular sectors may be constrained, and how the lack of development of these sectors affects the rest of the economy. Some sectors may be particularly useful in stimulating other sectors, by creating a demand for their products—what has been called backward linkages—and by supplying them with inputs, what has been called forward linkages, as stressed by Hirschman (1958). Some sectors may be particularly important for providing production experience, which generates technological improvements that can spill over into other sectors.

One sector which has received a great deal of attention is the agricultural sector, given its large size in the economy of many LDCs in terms of its share in total employment and total output, and the incidence of poverty in rural areas. It is argued that the sector is constrained by a variety of factors, including the system of land tenure, low levels of technology, and absence of irrigation and other infrastructure. Many have stressed institutional factors arising from the insecurity of tenure of tenants which prevents them from making long-term improvements in the land and the widespread use of sharecropping contracts which reduces the incentives of tenants to increase production. Especially farmers with very small landholdings are argued to be incapable of having access to technology and using scientific methods of cultivation, including the use of high-yielding varieties of seeds. Irrigation takes on the nature of public goods in the sense that if people from one farm cut a small canal or reservoir for irrigation purposes, others can use it, and this prevents any one of them from undertaking such projects. Governments can overcome such problems, but in LDCs local governments may not have the resources to undertake such projects because of the small amount of financial resources at their disposal.

If agricultural production does not expand, it is likely to create an obstacle for overall development, not only because of the large size of that sector in many LDCs, but also because its lack of development affects other sectors. For instance, if agriculture is stagnant and food prices are high, as stressed by W. Arthur Lewis (1954), in his highly influential dual economy model, workers in the manufacturing sector have to be paid higher wages to allow them to purchase the food to meet their basic needs (otherwise they will not be willing to work for wages in manufacturing and instead, remain in agriculture). This squeezes profits and reduces saving, investment, and capital accumulation, since profits are an important source of saving and investment. If the expansion of the manufacturing sector is held back by investment incentives rather than the supply of savings, high food prices due to a stagnant agriculture also make workers spend a large part of their income on food, and exert little demand for manufactured goods, resulting in a low market for such goods, which dampens investment incentives. Stagnation in agricultural production and income can also result in food insecurity, especially among the poor, and especially for countries which are unable to import food when needed, due to the lack of foreign exchange.

Manufacturing sectors have usually been viewed as the sectors which promote development in LDCs. Capital formation in manufacturing firms of various sizes has been viewed as important generators of income and employment and for yielding profits, which can be reinvested for further capital accumulation. They have also been seen as sectors which exhibit increasing returns (due to lower average costs of producing in bulk) and in which production experience and learning-by-doing results in technological change, which can spill over in other sectors, like other manufacturing sectors, agriculture, and services. Different types of manufacturing industries and industrial firms are viewed as having different types of advantages: high-technology and capital good sectors for generating technological change, and simple manufactured consumption goods sectors and small and medium-sized firms for generating employment and creating a demand for the products of sectors such as agriculture as intermediate inputs and for consumption goods demanded by workers. Very small informal sector firms, often hiring few or using only the labour of owners, may be too small for generating enough income for their owners and for reaping the benefits of scale economies.

The capital goods sector within manufacturing has attracted a great deal of attention from planners and policymakers in the early days of India's plans. In a closed economy, high growth through saving and investment not only requires devoting a high proportion of income to saving and investment rather than to consumption, but also the physical production of necessary amounts of capital or investment goods. This problem was stressed by the doyen of early Indian planners, P.C. Mahalanobis (1953), on the basis of a model similar to Feldman's model for Soviet planning, to justify the emphasis on the capital goods sector in India's Second Five Year Plan, which came into operation in the mid–1950s. The capital goods sector is unlikely to attract private investment in LDCs because of the uncertainty regarding profits, high installation costs, and complex and expensive technological needs. Even for an open economy, the lack of foreign exchange can limit the possibility of importing such goods, and the failure to build up these sectors has an adverse effect on technology development.

Another sector that has been emphasized is the infrastructure sector. In addition to irrigation in agriculture, important components of infrastructure include electrical power, transport, and communications facilities, all of which are important for production and marketing of goods and services. Like irrigation, they have public good characteristics, and they often do not attract much private investment because of high startup costs, which may take years to recoup, and for which the returns are highly uncertain. Governments usually take a leading role in building these sectors, but their ability to do so in LDCs is often constrained by the lack of financial resources, given their low taxable capacity.

Specific sectors can be supported by government policies including fiscal incentives such as subsidies, tax concessions, and government purchases. Other interventions include the subsidization of credit through government and other financial institutions (as done in South Korea), government assistance with sector-specific technological knowledge and inputs (such as in capital goods, technologically intensive manufacturing sectors, and genetically modified high-yielding seeds in agriculture, which has been an important component of what has been called the Green Revolution in many countries, including India), and in some cases by the establishment of state-owned enterprises where private investment is lacking (as in South Korea and India). For agriculture, improvements in conditions of land tenure and the redistribution of land with the imposition of land ceilings has been seen as improving both distribution by changing the ownership and pattern of use of land and as improving efficiency—by providing appropriate incentives to poor farmers (Banerjee, Gertler, and Ghatak 2002).

4

International Aspects
of Development

It is frequently asserted that countries are becoming increasingly interconnected. This phenomenon, usually referred to as globalization, is reflected by the increasing flows of goods and services, money, people, and ideas between countries, and is caused by a number of forces, including technological changes in transport and communications, changes in policies that control the level of interactions, and economic growth in many parts of the world. Our discussion of the economic aspects of development in the previous chapter, which assumed that the economy is a closed one in the sense that it does not interact with other countries, completely ignored this phenomenon, and therefore provided a necessarily incomplete view of the economic aspects of development.

It would seem that several of the obstacles to development discussed in the previous chapter can be overcome if one takes into account the economy's interaction with the rest of the world, for example, through international trade, payments, and technology transfers. For instance, the problem of inadequate capital accumulation due to low levels of saving can be overcome by borrowing internationally and paying back the loans after investments yield returns, or through foreign aid in the form of grants. Indeed, some analysts argue that by linking their economy to the global economy, LDCs can overcome many, if not all, of their development problems. However, others argue that many of the problems of LDCs actually arise in the relationship of the national economy to the world economy and that the development of LDCs is, in fact, constrained by these external problems. Thus, some argue that the influx of corporations from rich countries into LDCs destroys their domestic industries and leaks profits back to the richer countries rather than allowing capital accumulation in LDCs. We can examine these issues by discussing in turn international trade, international capital and labour flows, technology transfers, and some other forms of interaction.

International Trade

Many economists believe that trading with other countries fosters development in LDCs. There are many ways in which this can happen. Producers in LDCs can find markets for their products, overcoming the problem of aggregate demand for goods because of small markets within their borders caused by low levels of income, and the absence of domestic demand for some products (like crude oil) because they do not have the technology to process them for final use. LDCs can import goods and services from abroad when they are unable to produce them because they lack the resources and do not have the technological knowhow; thus, they can buy machinery and equipment abroad and set up industries which use them as capital goods.

Beyond these obvious ways, economists stress the benefits of specialization according to comparative advantage. Since countries have different amounts of various resources and differ in their technological capability of producing different things, they can produce some things better than others. Countries can, therefore, benefit from exporting those goods and services, in the production of which, because of their resources and technology, they are comparatively better suited. The argument based on technological differences was formalized by David Ricardo, an English classical economist in the nineteenth century, using the example of two countries, two goods, and one factor of production, labour. Suppose England and Portugal can both produce clothing and wine, but less labour is required to produce a unit of clothing in comparison to a unit of wine in the UK as compared to Portugal, then under conditions of the full utilization of labour in each country and free trade (that is, trade without government restrictions) in goods, Portugal will export wine to the UK and the latter will export clothing to the former. Moreover, both countries are likely to be better off in the sense of consuming a higher market value of the two goods. This will happen even if one country is absolutely more productive in producing both goods. This argument was later extended, in the twentieth century, by the Swedish economists Eli Heckscher and Bertil Ohlin, who focused on resource endowment differences between countries. To illustrate this approach suppose there are two goods, say airplanes and toys, which can be produced by two countries, say the US and China—using two factors of production, say high-skilled and low-skilled labour, which do not move internationally—and that the US has relatively more skilled labour than China, and airplane production makes more intensive use of skilled labour than toy production, which makes more intensive use of low-skilled labour. Then, if the two countries have identical technologies in the production of both goods (to abstract from Ricardo's argument for explaining comparative advantage) and similar demand patterns for the two goods, then the US will have a comparative advantage in producing planes and China in toys, trade will involve the US exporting planes to China and China exporting toys to the US, and both countries will be better off due to free trade than if they restricted trade or did not trade at all. These approaches highlight how countries, including LDCs, can allocate their resources better when they engage in free trade to maximize the value of goods and services available to them, and thereby, have higher levels of income and value of production and the resulting benefits that can come from that.

In addition, economists argue that exposing domestic producers to foreign competition—with imported goods and in global markets—can make them produce more efficiently, encourage innovation, and reduce their monopoly power, which keeps prices excessively high. Moreover, increasing trade allows countries to specialize more and thereby reap the advantages of large scale production rather than producing too many things at high costs. Finally, increasing trade can increase the exposure of LDCs to foreign goods, which may allow them to improve their own technology.

While there is much to be said for these development benefits from international trade, these arguments and the theories on which they are based ignore a number of issues. Consider, for instance, the Ricardian and Heckscher-Ohlin approaches, which continue to underpin most economists' thinking about trade between rich and poor countries. Among other characteristics, these theories are static in the sense of taking factor (or input) endowments and technology as given rather than changing over time; they also assume that all factors are fully utilized, and that trade is balanced between countries and individual countries can trade any amount they want to at given world prices (the so-called small country assumption).

If we depart from the static framework, problems can arise for LDCs. Education and skill formation can suffer in LDCs. If the assumptions of the Heckscher-Ohlin-Samuelson approach are satisfied, the expansion of trade leads to the increase in the production of goods in which countries have a comparative advantage. The result is an increase in the price of factors of production used intensively in these industries, that is, their abundant factor, since the demand for that factor increases at home with the growth of production at the expense of imports. Since LDCs are relatively abundant in low-skilled labour and high-income countries are relatively abundant in high-skilled labour, the high-skilled wage will rise in the rich country and fall in the poor countries. This can increase incentives for obtaining education to increase skills in rich countries and to reduce them in poor countries. Thus, if growth is positively affected by an expansion of education, and to the extent that education improves individual functioning, development may be hampered in LDCs due to trade liberalization. Moreover, comparative advantage is likely to make rich countries specialize in more technologically sophisticated goods and services and poor countries specialize in products that are simpler, and to the extent that experience in the production of the former type of good results in greater technological learning, trade is likely to slow down technological change in poor countries. Thus, increasing international trade can bring about short-term benefits but cause long-run developmental problems.

Further, when trade increases due to the reduction of trade barriers, the production of some goods, those in which the country does not have a comparative advantage, falls and people and other factors of production that are employed in these sectors will not be used any more. This is not a problem because under the assumptions of the theory—that all factors are fully utilized due to changes in the price of these factors—they will be employed in other sectors which would be expanding production, including that for exports. If, however, we depart from the assumptions that all factors are fully utilized and that countries may not be able to export whatever they want to at the going world price (because the world demand for their products is limited due to low quality and the lack of market penetration abroad), unemployment and underemployment can increase. Moreover, if we depart from the assumption that international trade is balanced, the country can run a trade deficit, that is, it can find that it imports more than it exports, which is possible by borrowing from abroad. If they are limited in their access to foreign credit or other forms of foreign capital inflows, and therefore foreign exchange is limited, they may have to reduce their imports of those goods which can allow them to increase their production and grow faster, for example, intermediate materials like oil or capital goods. We will have more to say about trade deficits and international capital movements later.

For now, we can add that trade liberalization can be problematic if it results in poor countries continuing to specialize in a few simple manufactured goods or primary products: they are likely to face a long-run deterioration and volatility in their terms of trade, which can cause fluctuations and long-term worsening of their foreign exchange positions. Many of their products, especially primary goods and traditional manufacturing exports, often face limited world markets because the demand for them does not increase by much when world income increases (they have what economists call a low income elasticity of demand). Although there is some controversy regarding this, the terms of trade for LDCs—the average price they receive for their exports as a ratio of the average price they pay for their imports—has shown a general tendency to decline if one leaves out some specific goods like petroleum, which has exacerbated the problem of trade imbalances. This has been called the Prebisch-Singer hypothesis, after two pioneering development economists who first emphasized these problems in the 1950s (Singer 1950; Prebisch 1950). The result has been shortages of foreign exchange which, by limiting imports of essential capital and intermediate goods, has restricted growth. Also, the volatility of the terms of trade in response to fluctuations in world market conditions creates problems for those LDCs which specialize in the exports of a few goods, given the fact that they are sold in markets which are competitive and hence subject to large price fluctuations, and sometimes also subject to speculative price changes.

International trade can also have adverse effects on the environment in LDCs. Since LDCs typically adopt and enforce fewer environmental regulations, it is likely that they have a comparative advantage in the production of goods which cause more environmental damage, and the expansion of these sectors can exacerbate environmental degradation, which results in developmental problems.

Belief in the benefits of free trade leads to the policy prescription of removing trade restrictions in the form of import tariffs and quotas in order to maximize the benefits from trade. International organizations, such as The World Bank, International Monetary Fund (IMF), and especially the World Trade Organization (WTO), promote trade liberalization and bind LDCs to reducing import tariffs. However, the problem with generalized trade liberalization is that it can lead to the kinds of development problems we have just discussed. Many LDCs, especially those in Latin America and Africa, have experienced industrial contraction because of such trade liberalization (Stiglitz 2002; Chang 2007). It should come as no surprise that most developed countries of today—including England, the US, Germany, Japan, and South Korea—have, in the past, adopted restrictive trade policies to promote their industrial development (Chang 2007). For instance, in its early days of industrialization, England adopted protectionist policies at home, to protect its nascent textiles industries, while forcing free trade and open markets on its colonies, like the US and India, to expand its exports, and later on the US and Germany adopted protectionist measures to allow them to challenge British industrial dominance. It is interesting to note that the countries in Ricardo's own example, England and Portugal, experienced very divergent development patterns, something than can, in part, be explained by their pattern of trade specialization which, incidentally, resulted from England's military successes and enforced agreements rather than free trade.

In recent years, many LDCs have experienced considerable increases in the export of finished manufactured goods and have become involved in the production and export of intermediate goods and the assembly of final products using imported intermediate goods, as parts of what are called global production networks. This increase in the production and exports of manufactures goods, however, does not seem to have changed the basic structure of trading relations between the North and the South, with the latter producing mostly simpler manufactured goods and technologically less sophisticated intermediates and performing simple assembly operations.

International Capital Flows

International capital inflows—involving foreign borrowing, especially from rich countries—can support economic development in LDCs by allowing them to supplement their domestic saving to increase investment, capital accumulation, and growth, and to increase the foreign exchange available to them to allow them to import necessary intermediate inputs and capital goods for expanding output and investment. Moreover, access to international borrowing can allow LDCs to overcome problems due to output and income fluctuations—from weather conditions or terms of trade fluctuations—by borrowing when times are bad and paying back when times are good, avoiding painful and inefficient consumption and investment volatility. Capital inflows can take various forms, such as bank borrowing, the purchase of stocks and bonds issued in LDCs by foreigners, or what is called portfolio capital flows, and foreign direct investment, when foreign entities, usually transnational corporations, bring in funds and maintain control over what is done with the funds, for instance, by setting up production units in LDCs.

The problem with these lines of reasoning is that, as is often observed, capital does not move much from rich to poor countries, and that international capital tends not to move when it is most needed by poor countries, that is, during bad times. Although, it may be expected that capital will move internationally from capital-abundant rich countries to capital-scarce poor countries, in fact, flows of capital from rich to poor countries is rather limited and confined to a few LDCs that are already doing well. The reason for this has been argued to be the lack of adequate infrastructure, education, and other resources in LDCs, which keeps the return to capital low, and the problem poor-country borrowers have in convincing rich-country lenders that they are not too risky, partly because of the lack of suitable collateral and the possibility of default. Moreover, many poor countries, such as China, seek to protect themselves against foreign exchange problems due to external and internal shocks by holding large stocks of liquid assets issued by rich countries such as the US, thereby lending to these rich countries. Finally, some economists argue that poor countries are unable to attract foreign capital because of government policies, ranging from those which impose restrictions on capital flows, such as not allowing foreigners to buy stocks and imposing taxes on such flows, to those which create a generally inhospitable climate for foreign investors by over-regulating the financial sector and the economy in general.

Moreover, capital flows, especially bank lending and portfolio flows, tend to be volatile and pro-cyclical. When times are good, there is usually a surge in capital inflows, which sometimes move into real estate and stock markets, causing asset market booms rather than financing productive investment. This problem, which is arguably endemic to financial markets everywhere, is particularly problematic for poor countries which do not have large financial markets that can absorb the shocks and international financial flows where the problem of uncertainty and the possibility of moving funds to other countries are large. Large inflows, in addition to creating destabilizing asset bubbles, result in exchange rate appreciation, which make a country's exports less competitive and imports cheaper, worsening the trade deficit, and the resultant outflows necessitate contractionary policies which reduce economic growth and government 'social' spending on the poor, which, in turn, adversely affects poverty and

112

inequality. Policies that have been recommended to deal with these problems include careful regulation and supervision and even government ownership of banks and other financial institutions, macroeconomic management (of fiscal and monetary policy), which is anti-cyclical in nature, that is, following contractionary policies when capital flows in and expansionary policies when it flows out, and restrictions on international capital flows.

Given the volatility of these kinds of flows, LDC governments have shown a preference for foreign direct investment (FDI). Not only can FDI inflows be a more stable source of foreign capital, which increases saving and foreign exchange availability, but they can also bring in better technology and managerial methods, directly increase investment (when it is in the form of what is called 'greenfield' investment, that is, creating of new production facilities), promote exports (given the global market presence of the transnational corporation involved), reduce imports of those goods which can be produced in the country by these corporations, and promote competition by challenging the monopoly power of domestic firms. These gains, however, are not guaranteed, as stressed earlier by the 'dependency' theorists in the 1960s and 1970s. FDI can be an important conduit of technology transfer from abroad because transnational corporations can bring in advanced technology, and these improvements can spill over into domestic firms because of the mobility of workers between transnational and domestic firms and due to subcontracting relationships, where domestic firms have to meet quality standards to supply inputs to transnational firms. However, these corporations often engage in assembly production without bringing in, revealing, and developing new technology, and bring in technology inappropriate to LDC conditions (for example, mechanized methods when there is need for labour intensive methods for employment growth). Transnational corporations have, therefore, at times been criticized for creating enclaves which are virtually part of the more developed country where it is headquartered rather than the LDCs where they are located, and having few linkages with the rest of the economy of the latter through increasing the demand for inputs and technological spillovers. FDI is often in the form of acquisitions of existing firms and can also harm firms by competing with them, thereby

114

not increasing investment. They can result in a large increase in imports of intermediate goods and sales of their products internally rather than for exports, which implies, when one takes into account the repatriation of profits, that the foreign exchange implication of FDI is unfavourable. They can also monopolize sectors into which they enter, rather than encouraging competition. Finally, they can introduce the more environment-polluting production processes in LDCs, where environmental regulations are weaker and less strictly applied, exacerbating, in the process, environmental problems in such countries.

Governments can increase the positive linkages and weaken the negative effects through appropriate policies which include restrictions on the sectoral allocation of investment in order to direct it into high-technology sectors, by actively encouraging technology transfer agreements to domestic affiliates, by imposing export and domestic content requirements, and by helping in the creation of an educated labour force. Global competition and international agreements—for instance, the trade related investment measures (TRIMs) agreement of the WTO—limits the ability of most

LDC governments to pursue such policies. They are not impossible to pursue, especially for large countries and for groups of smaller countries that cooperate with each other. Not many LDCs receive large amounts of FDI, and when they do, FDI seems to follow growth (arguably due to expanding markets and the spread of education and labour skills) rather than, except in a few cases, causing development. Reducing regulations on FDI often does not have a positive effect on inflows; many countries which have relaxed such regulations without experiencing some prior economic improvements have received little or no FDI.

International Labour Movements

Labour movements across countries, especially from LDCs to rich countries, are highly restricted by immigration policies in the latter and when there is some movement, it is biased towards high-skilled workers with low-skilled labour migration, often undocumented, occurring mostly in countries with contiguous borders (as in migration from Mexico to the US). The movement of high-skilled workers, who receive education in LDCs and then migrate to rich countries where they receive higher wages, is often seen as a problem of the brain drain for poor countries, slowing down technological change and growth (for instance, due to the departure of scientists and engineers), as well as having an adverse effect on health and education (due to the emigration of health professionals and teachers). However, for many LDCs, emigrants transfer a large amount of remittances, which improves the country of origin's balance of payments (as in the cases of India and Mexico) and health and education conditions (by augmenting their family resources and, sometimes, by pooling funds to establish schools in their home areas). However, such inflows often increase inequality and result in increases in conspicuous consumption rather than in improving functionings and investment for growth. Moreover, it has been argued that successful diaspora entrepreneurs and engineers living abroad can improve the image of their country of origin and thereby increase exports (as seems to have happened for the information technology sector in India), and also bring about an increase in FDI and portfolio inflows.

Technology Transfers

Technology transfers from rich to poor countries provide an excellent opportunity to the latter for improving their technology and experiencing growth without having to reinvent the figurative wheel. Indeed, many countries that are now more developed initially imported foreign technology to catch up with those which were technologically more advanced. It has been argued that the speed of technology transfers depends on the gap between the level of foreign technology and domestic technology, since the potential to learn is greater. Some commentators argue that technology transfers from high-income to low-income countries will enable low-income countries to catch up in terms of productivity.

However, it may not be a simple matter to transfer technology since, as anyone who has been a student knows, it is necessary to have the prerequisites to obtain further knowledge. Much of this knowledge is tacit, rather than fully codified, it needs to be adapted to local conditions and applications require the ability to detect and overcome problems, and these problems have become more severe as the complexity of technology has grown (Amsden 2001). To make use of this knowledge effectively, therefore, requires not only an improvement in skills through education, but also the development of what has been called technological capability, which requires, among other things, experience in producing increasingly more technologically sophisticated goods and the creation of research and development facilities. Thus, the diffusion of technology across borders is not fundamentally different from the process of innovation (Bell and Pavitt 1993). Transnational corporations can bring in foreign technology and are often a major conduit for technology transfers, but little of this takes place if the corporations mainly engage in assembly and low-technology manufacturing to take advantage of low wages or if they jealously guard their more advanced proprietary technology. Moreover, the international extension of patents and other intellectual property rights protection, for instance through the trade related intellectual property rights (TRIPs) agreement of the WTO, has raised the costs and possibilities of technology transfers to LDCs, a problem that countries which tried to industrialize by liberally transferring foreign technology in the past did not have to face (Chang

2007). It is unlikely that the Indian pharmaceutical industry could have grown as much as it did in the past if it had to abide by international agreements regarding patents before the TRIPs agreement was implemented.

Some Broader Issues

Beyond the interactions just discussed, international factors affect development in LDCs in other, broader, ways. Closer links to rich countries through television, internet, and other media, and through travel and the presence of transnational corporations, has cultural effects on attitudes, norms, and preferences of people in LDCs. For instance, the observation of consumerist lifestyles in rich countries can lead to a reduction of saving rates in poor countries through the so-called international demonstration effect and to a preference for foreign brand names in consumer goods, increasing imports and the importance of transnational corporations in the economy. Competition in global markets can make LDC governments relax regulations on environmental pollution and working conditions and wages, leading to a race to the bottom to maintain and enhance international competitiveness.

International influences can also affect the nature of government policies in LDCs. Rich country governments which provide foreign aid and market access, transnational corporations which sometimes have strong bargaining power because of their large size, and international organizations like the IMF, The World Bank, and the WTO, can have a major influence on policies that have significant development impacts on LDCs. These include lowering barriers to free trade and financial capital flows, reducing restrictions on the activities of transnational corporations, and the protection of intellectual property rights internationally. Although LDCs join the international organizations voluntarily and seem eager to join them because of the benefits from membership—such as obtaining access to rich country markets and help with international financing—the fact that they are dominated by rich countries either formally or informally frequently induce these countries to adopt policies which may not be in the best interests of their people. This is not to say that these policies are imposed on LDCs by overt force as they were in colonial times, or that the policies do not have the support of some domestic groups, but they tilt the balance towards their adoption.

These comments have made us go beyond narrow economic forces by discussing aspects of political economy. It is time we examined non–economic issues more systematically.

5

Non-economic Aspects of Development

Many social scientists and, increasingly, more economists are looking beyond the boundaries of narrowly
defined economics to examine other obstacles to
development. Non-economists have long emphasized
climatic, political, social, and cultural obstacles to
development. For instance, the lack of development
has been related to cultural habits and practices that
discourage saving, investment, and entrepreneurial
activity, create a general apathy towards the pursuit of
material goals and militate against a 'rational' world
view, to political problems such as the behaviour of
despotic rulers who have little interest in economic
progress and impoverish their subjects with heavy
taxes, and political instability and violent conflict.

Many scholars also argue that years of colonial rule created conditions that perpetuate the lack of development. Economists have recently taken a greater interest in traditionally non-economic obstacles, distinguishing between what some call 'proximate' causes of growth and development which relate to such issues as capital accumulation through saving and investment, and technological change on the one hand, and 'fundamental' causes on the other; among the latter, geography and institutions, closely related to political and social factors, have received increasing attention. In this chapter, we examine some 'non-economic' obstacles to development, although keeping in mind the fact that it is not obvious where the boundary between the economic and the non-economic lies.

History

Historical explanations of underdevelopment have the common feature of pointing to some events in the past that created conditions favouring development in some places and the lack of development in others, and arguing that these conditions tend to persist over time. They differ in what specific events or conditions explain the initial difference, that is, the original 'virtue' or 'sin', so to speak, and what forces explain the persistence, perpetuation, or even exacerbation of these differences. They also differ in the extent to which they see the original event and the persistence of its effects to be related to the interaction between the differentially affected places.

Regarding initial events, it has been claimed by some observers that events in Europe, such as the Black Death which raised wages by reducing labour supplies and thereby induced labour-saving technological changes, or changes in religious attitudes due to the Protestant Reformation, which favoured hard work and thrift and resulted a new view of the relationship between humans and nature, and fostered technological innovation, brought about economic improvements in parts of Europe, changes which did not occur elsewhere. While these explanations do not involve interactions between different parts of the world, other explanations—such as those which stress the role of colonization and involve the plunder and the looting of resources, forced trade in goods and people as slaves, and imposition of foreign rule and policies and institutions inimical to development in colonized regions, for instance, bring about patterns of trade specialization that made colonies export primary products and import manufactured goods—emphasize interactions due to which some regions of the world benefited and others were hurt (Bagchi 2005).

Examples of mechanisms of persistence include the purely economic one of increasing returns according to which increased production leads to lower average costs and greater efficiency, to broader ones involving political economy and institutional factors. If some regions of the world go ahead (due to 'initial' events) in the production of those types of goods that generate higher productivity growth, they experience improvements in their economic position as they are able to produce more and out-compete other regions that find themselves specializing in the production of simpler goods which do not generate such scale economies; thus, slight initial advantages can lead to a widening gap over time that become difficult to reverse (Dutt 1990). Some regions that follow a certain path may be locked into that path due to what has been called network externalities—self-reinforcing social tendencies which make individuals and firms do things in a way that make them continue along that path rather than follow more efficient alternatives. An example of lock-in is the continued use of the QWERTY keyboard in preference to the DVORAK format which is supposed to be more efficient in terms of typing speed, because people are habituated to using that system and producers and technicians are experienced in producing and repairing them (David 1985). The powerful groups which benefit from such a denouement can successfully push for the adoption of policies which maintain the status quo. For instance, powerful traders who reap profits from international trading activities may successfully oppose policy changes that increase domestic production and restrict international trade, as in the case of Latin America (Bulmer-Thomas 1994).

Mechanisms such as these strengthen the case for the careful study of historical events and processes which make their results persist over time, but do not imply that it is impossible to come out of the shadows of history. Some countries have escaped situations of poverty and economic backwardness, and it may be possible to weaken the mechanisms which result in the persistence of poverty resulting from historical events. However, greater awareness of historical events and processes can point to the difficulties involved in, and provide guidance on, what can be done to overcome the negative forces of persistence.

Geography

Favourable geographical conditions, such as fertile soil and favourable weather conditions allowed people in prehistory to increase their production of crops and domesticate animals, thereby launching civilizations which could produce well beyond their basic (food) needs (Diamond 1997). However, many regions which enjoyed these conditions, such as the fertile crescent of the Middle East, did not pioneer what is widely considered to be modern economic development. Nevertheless, a look at the world map does suggest some role for geography: many of today's LDCs are located close to the equator, and many more developed countries are found in temperate zones some distance from it. Possible obstacles to economic development include: hot weather which makes people unable to work hard and provides breeding grounds for diseases which lead to bad health and morbidity and, hence, low productivity; and the property of being land-locked, which hampers oceanic trade. Paradoxically, geography can also kill with kindness: for instance good weather, fertile land, and abundant natural resources can make some parts of the world become self-sufficient, complacent, and insular and become easy prey to outsiders who, lacking such 'good' fortune, had to look outwards and develop their military prowess in order to plunder and loot through conquest and domination, creating the colonial nexus mentioned earlier. Moreover, the abundance of resources, even today, leads people to fight each other to grab their share of the extractable bounty, while others who are not cursed by the existence of resources have to engage in productive activity, paving the way to economic development.

Institutions

Of late, it has become fashionable in mainstream economics to argue that institutions are the fundamental determinants of growth and development (Acemoglu and Robinson 2012). The role of institutions in blocking development has, however, been long emphasized by many economists and other social scientists, such as Gunnar Myrdal, who are called institutional economists.

The word institutions has been used in many senses, and sometimes described as the 'rules of the game' in which individuals and groups in society operate. They are most usefully defined as comprising of laws and formal rules; informal habits, social norms, or conventions which affect how people and groups behave, especially with each other; and more or less formal organizations of people or groups. Laws and rules include statutes, bodies of case law, and constitutions. Informal norms and conventions can be ingrained habits, though all habits are not norms and conventions, only those that are more or less widely shared. Organizations include the courts, the police, civil service bureaucracies, firms, trade unions, families, and official international organizations. The need for combining these three aspects of society into one concept comes from the fact that it is impossible to understand each one and its role in the economy without understanding the others.

In much of the mainstream economics literature the institutional obstacle that has been emphasized most in recent years is that of the absence of well-defined private property rights. Although the literature has stressed other institutions as well, such as those which promote market freedom and market flexibility, establish democracy (which we will discuss later), improve governance, and reduce corruption, a flavour of the issues involved regarding institutions can be obtained with a brief discussion of private property rights. The establishment of private property rights has been seen as a precondition for development since, it is argued, that if property rights are not protected, economic agents will have little incentive to produce, trade, save, and invest, fearing that what they obtain from these activities will be appropriated by others, including the state. Moreover, it is argued that the absence of well-defined property rights over resources which is open for use to all results in what has been called the tragedy of the commons. People use them beyond what is required to maintain them for future use, because they believe if they do not, others will do so, leaving them nothing for the future; examples include forest resources and fish stocks. It is also argued that without the protection of intellectual property rights, such as patents, which give innovators monopoly power by at least temporarily stopping unauthorized copying by competitors, the incentives for innovation would disappear or at least decline, slowing down technological change.

While the case for private property for providing incentives for saving, investment, and growth is a strong one, the issue is complex. The concept of private property rights involves many dimensions, including the right of access without subtractive benefits, the right to withdraw products, the right to manage and to improve, the right to exclude others from access and withdrawal and acceptable methods of doing so, and the right to sell exclusion rights; different configurations of these dimensions may have different effects depending on how they affect the degree of control rather than some definition of ownership of the appropriate decision makers (Rodrik 2007). Again, for property rights, formal rules can never be completely specified but require interpretation by the courts, their compliance depends on both social norms and enforcement by organizations, and changes in rules may well result in changes in norms that reduce the control of relevant owners. In some cases, as mentioned in Chapter 3, the imposition of private property rights can be harmful for efficiency when they replace informal institutional arrangements that have been developed over long periods of time to deal with common property resources (Ostrom 1990).

Moreover, attempts to secure property rights (as well as promoting market freedoms) can have undesirable consequences because the real world is unlikely to satisfy the stringent conditions that market economies need to satisfy for the first welfare theorem to hold, which, as we discussed in Chapter 3, is the basis for much of the mainstream approach. Externalities, asymmetric information, and various kinds of market power abound in many economies (which institutional changes are unlikely to overcome), especially in LDCs; uncertainty renders the entire theoretical apparatus of mainstream economics problematic.

The need for some kinds of private property rights, such as those related to intellectual property, is especially problematic. In theoretical terms it is not clear that patents and other intellectual property right protection speed up innovation: while they can provide greater monetary rewards for innovation, they also raise the costs of innovation by reducing access to the fruits of other innovations which can serve as inputs into innovative activity, and it diverts resources from innovative activity to the protection of intellectual property rights through legal means. There is, indeed, little empirical evidence to suggest that intellectual property rights protection actually speeds up innovation (Boldrin and Levine 2008). The problem posed by the world–wide spread of intellectual property rights is particularly severe for LDCs for which technological change, to a large extent, involves transferring technology developed in more developed countries.

Finally, institutions can have different effects regarding different goals of development. Property rights strengthen a kind of rights, and their effect on efficiency and growth has been emphasized in the mainstream discussion. But they also affect distribution and functionings such as being adequately nourished, which are, in turn, related to efficiency and growth. For instance, as mentioned in Chapter 3, land reforms which violate the private property rights of some and redistribute land and thereby extend private property rights for a large group of people can improve asset and income distribution, while also increasing efficiency in agricultural production.

Political Factors

Almost everyone agrees that the state (and its components, including politicians in government, the judiciary and police, the military, and the civil service) has a positive role to play in development. Some stress its role in maintaining law and order, providing national defence, enforcing contracts, establishing and protecting various types of property rights, and creating a general environment in which private enterprise can flourish. Others go further and argue that it has a role in overcoming market failures, for instance, due to externalities, the existence of public goods, monopolies, and imperfect information (see Chapter 3). Yet others argue that the existence of uncertainty prevents private individuals and organizations from performing activities like building up key industries, so that the state has to provide a helping hand or even develop the industries with state-owned enterprises. It is argued by many that the state can and should improve the well-being of those who are left in poverty or are exposed to various kinds of insecurities by market and social forces. However, political leaders may be unwilling or unable to perform these roles, and may even create barriers to development by attempting to enrich themselves at the expense of the rest of society. When the state acts in this way (or when other non-state political institutions such as political parties fail to function appropriately) we can say that they create political obstacles to development.

The most obvious example of a political obstacle is a state which lacks the power to perform the tasks just mentioned even at the most basic level. Such states, sometimes referred to as 'failed states', lack the coercive power, organization, and legitimacy to provide basic services, such as maintaining basic law and order and keeping transport systems in workable order, let alone foster development. In some cases, this lack of power manifests itself in political instability, accompanied by civil conflict. The result is a situation in which the future is extremely uncertain and in which private incentives are at low levels and the state can do little directly; a vicious cycle is created which weakens the state further. But political obstacles can exist under less extreme conditions. It is useful to analyse such obstacles in terms of three aspects of the political system of a country, although they are closely related: the objectives of the state and its components; the relationship of the state to the society at large; and the organization of the state and other political institutions.

The objectives of the state and its components may include personal enrichment and empowerment, maintaining its power, improving the conditions of those in society who are associated to them, and broader developmental goals. These objectives, of course, may not be mutually exclusive: for instance, an effective way of maintaining power is by pursuing development goals and winning general approval. However, it is worth keeping such varied objectives in mind to avoid the narrow and cynical view that those in power merely try to enrich themselves through corrupt practices or the naive one that they work only for the common good. In some countries, states have been clearly predatory and extractive and enriched political leaders at the expense of society at large, and in others, such as in South Korea and Taiwan, it has been argued to be developmentalist (Evans 1989). In India, the state seems to have both developmentalist and corrupt sides. While corruption and rent-seeking may have pernicious developmental effects, for instance by siphoning off resources away from productive uses and by increasing the incentives for unproductive behaviour, it need not do so if, for instance, corruption directs resources to those whose success leads to industrialization and export growth, or if the personal aggrandizement or the political power of leaders requires them to share their gains with the society at large, especially with the poor.

The relationship of the state to the society at large requires an examination of different groups in society, which can be called classes, interest groups, or coalitions, and how they are related to those who occupy important positions in different components of the state. These groups can influence the state through political support in the form of votes and other demonstrations of political support, financial contributions, and direct representation in governments. Those groups in society who have more influence on the state can try to push forward policies and institutions which, they perceive, will further their own interests and block those that they perceive will hurt them. Thus, what the state does or does not do reflects both the power and interests of different groups, and the effect of the state on development depends on how what the state does actually promotes development.

In some situations, groups that are numerically strong can affect government policies by how they vote, their opinions as reflected in polls, and through social movements. In other situations those who are better organized because they are smaller and more cohesive, so that they are able to overcome what Mancur Olson (1965) has called the problem of collective action due to the free rider problem, have greater influence. Usually, though, money talks and the powerful groups are the ones with more income and wealth, because they can buy the support of others in society, influence government officials directly, and organize themselves better. If the interest of powerful groups lie in increasing their share of income and maintaining their power, they are likely to block changes such as those which reduce income inequality which, as we have seen in Chapter 3, are likely to have a positive effect on economic development. Sometimes power relations may be more complex. Pranab Bardhan (1984) has analysed the Indian situation and identified the dominant groups as being: the industrial capitalists whose power is based on their disproportionate ownership and control of industrial capital; large and medium landowners, whose power is based on the ownership of land; and the educated elites who exercise control over higher education and various elements of the state bureaucracy. He argues that while each of these groups is powerful, they are not powerful enough to pursue their interests alone and have to form coalitions and appease each other, and exercise multiple veto powers to block policy changes and implementation. Examples of such policies (or their absence) have been argued to include: the expansion of subsidies to the dominant groups, which reduces the ability of the state to increase investment or improve the conditions of the poor; the neglect of land reform in many parts of the country to placate landowners; the maintenance of a large range of government regulations to make it easier for bureaucrats to benefit from corruption; to protect big business against foreign competition; and to maintain a relatively closed education system to maintain a high income for those with more education. These configurations of the relationship between the state and dominant groups do not imply that no developmentist policies are possible. Changes can indeed take place when the state is very strong (and relatively autonomous from societal pressures), paradoxically, when the state is very weak and throws caution to the wind, when dominant groups have large internal divisions, and when it is supported by strong groups whose interests and broader social interests are closely aligned (Kohli 2004). However, the analysis implies that societal pressures may make it difficult for the state to promote development even when it is willing to do so.

Finally, the organization of the state and other political institutions can have an important impact on development prospects. One debate is about the relative merits of democracies and authoritarian regimes: some argue that the authoritarian Chinese system has been far more successful in promoting development, both in the sense of reducing poverty and improving human development indicators and in promoting growth, than India's democratic system, while others are convinced that India has a brighter future because of its democratic polity while the Chinese authoritarian system is on the brink of collapse. While democracies are intrinsically more appealing because of the greater political freedom they typically allow, no clear relationship has been found to exist between economic growth or economic development defined more broadly and whether economies are more or less democratic, but democracies seem to have a smaller amount of variation in performance.

A number of reasons have been cited for why democracies may have an advantage over authoritarian regimes. For one, democracies are better at resolving conflicts by recourse to the ballot box, than authoritarian regimes, where the main way in which governments change is by violent conflict which, through death, physical destruction of capital and infrastructure, creating greater uncertainty, and by diverting resources to conflict rather than productive activity, blocks development. Also, democracies are more likely to provide better information to, and result in greater accountability among, government officials, and involve most of society in having greater 'ownership' of policy interventions, helping their implementation. For instance, as Amartya Sen (1999) has argued, famines are far less likely to occur in democracies rather than in authoritarian regimes, because a free press is more likely to provide information about problems and hold politicians and government bureaucrats more accountable in overcoming the worst consequences of famines, for instance, with the government distributing food to famine-afflicted areas. Beyond simply providing more information, public discussion and debate is more likely to result in a more well-reasoned crystallization and articulation of the will of the people. Finally, governments in democracies are likely to be more responsive to the will of the people, and pursue policies which are more likely to improve the well-being of the majority of the people.

The general applicability of such claims, however, is open to question. First, democracies need not resolve conflicts peacefully. There are cases in which after inequality grows due to a minority becoming richer because of their privileged economic and political positions, the majority can oust them from political power through elections, inducing the more powerful minority to retaliate by subverting democratic processes (Chua 2004). Second, democracies are likely to favour policies which focus on the short term because politicians seeking reelection want to show quick results. Third, while democracies may have a role in reducing the chances of the occurrence of catastrophic events such as famines, they may not be able to reduce less catastrophic but debilitating problems such as long-term malnutrition simply because the latter does not make good press, as Sen has conceded. Finally, with large wealth and income inequalities, democracies can make governments less responsive to the needs of the poor and the politically weak, by muting their 'voice' in public discussion and debate. Moreover, because of political inertia discussed earlier, the development efforts of the state may be constrained.

In addition to the effect of general concepts like democracy, other more specific issues about the political and governance system, including the extent of decentralization of the government, the nature of the civil service, and the characteristics of political parties, can have an effect of development. Like the debate on democracy, there are no clear answers here. For instance, decentralization in governance can lead to better results by involving the people most affected by policies to have a say in shaping and successfully implementing changes, but it is possible that local governments are more susceptible to capture by local elites. In general, however, states are more successful with development policies when civil service bureaucrats as in South Korea (or political parties as in Taiwan) have what Peter Evans (1995) calls 'embedded autonomy' that is, they are sufficiently embedded in society to understand what is needed for development 'on the ground' and are trusted by private sector groups, while being relatively autonomous and not overly influenced and constrained by powerful groups.

Social and Cultural Factors

The attitudes and behaviour of individuals are obviously affected by social factors which influence how they act individually and how they interact with each other. A long tradition claims that certain types of attitudes and behaviour are conducive to development and others are detrimental to it, and that these attitudes and norms—which can be thought of as an aspect of institutions as mentioned earlier—are often determined by shared religious beliefs. For instance, Max Weber (1930) stressed the role of the Protestant ethic in creating conditions for the rise of capitalism and economic progress, by encouraging hard work, saving and capital accumulation, and a general desire to improve one's position in this world rather than focusing on the afterlife. Not all such norms and attitudes are based on religious beliefs, however; they can be related to culture more generally, which refers to patterns of meanings that include actions, sayings, and meaningful objects through which individuals communicate with each other and share their ideas, experiences, and values. Colonial administrators and those believing in modernization theories argued that traditional values that stress spending on religious and cultural activities rather than on investment and limited material needs, downright indolence, and dishonesty create obstacles to development. It was often argued that non-western societies remained in poverty because of their social norms which militated against accumulation, work, trading, and business activity.

It has often been claimed that culture in general and religious values in particular have constrained development in many parts of the world, including Latin America, China, and the Islamic world. The Indian economy's low rate of growth used to be called the Hindu rate of growth and at least one book about the Indian economy referred to India's development problems as a Hindu equilibrium (Lal 2004). Earlier writers had attributed the problems to Hinduism's stress on the afterlife and preoccupation with the doctrine of karma, which made people accept their lot as a punishment for sins in past lives rather than overcome their poverty through purposeful action, and to accept inequality and poverty among others on similar terms (Morris 1967). Particular emphasis has been placed on the caste system, which has been argued to reduce economic mobility, reduce expectations and incentives for economic advancement, and the acceptance of inequality (Nair 1962). Members of higher caste elites have held political and economic power and maintained a firm grip on education which, it has been argued, led to a neglect of basic education and to an improvement of higher education which has not led to economic development because of the lack of jobs which can utilize the skills of those with higher education. Moreover, neoliberal economists have argued that it has created a culture in which people of higher castes who are part of the economic and political elites have held the view that other castes have to be controlled and regulated for their own good and for the good of the nation as a whole, thereby encouraging a government-controlled economy (Lal 2004).

The argument that religious and other factors are embodied in norms that block development has a number of problems. It has been observed that values can change in response to other factors, sometimes quite quickly. For instance, many norms, such as those which result in low labour productivity and corruption, are the result of poverty and the absence of development, and not so much the cause of them, and can change when economic conditions change. Cultures have many aspects to them and it is easy to overstress the role of certain aspects of them and to ignore others which may be more favourable about development. For instance, it has been claimed that Islamic culture is, on the one hand fixated on afterlife and violent jihad rather than materialist pursuits, and on the other, is supportive of business and trading (the Prophet Mohammed himself was a merchant) and, as such, has a well-developed sense of contracts (Chang 2007). Moreover economic behaviour, policies, and institutions are not just affected by cultural values but also power relations, economic conditions, and the outcome of academic and policy debates. Finally, the effects of social norms need not be the same everywhere. High saving rates may be good for some economies, but not necessarily for others in which investment incentives and growing aggregate demand are of great importance.

It is not surprising, then, that there are so many ex-post explanations of economic performance and policies in terms of values, and so many incorrect ex-ante predictions based on them (Chang 2007). For instance, Weber argued that the Confucian ethic was a barrier to economic growth in explaining East Asia's economic stagnation, Morishima (1982) argued that the Japanese version of Confucianism was conducive to development and the Chinese version is not after Japan developed, and now many people relate China's high growth to China's Confucian ethic because it stresses social order and the importance of education and training.

There are some social factors that continue to be emphasized by some social scientists, including the importance of what has been called social capital. Social capital refers the collection of social networks which can benefit individuals among whom connections are strong, and can benefit entire groups and societies. The importance of social capital has been emphasized not only for the smooth operation of markets by promoting trust between trading parties that overcome the problem of opportunistic violations of agreements and contracts, but also for reducing conflict and promoting cooperation among people in organizations which are not based on market principles, for instance, in firms, the success and productivity of which arguably depend on harmonious relationships. Suggestions have been made for increasing interactions between different people and the fostering of social organizations and communities. However, such claims sometimes ignore the nature of interactions and relations between different people within the relevant entities, such as firms, their relative power, and their possibly opposed economic interests.

6

Strategies for Economic Development

What strategies can be adopted by governments and other organizations to foster economic development in LDCs? What are the merits and disadvantages of alternative strategies? What have been the policy experiences of LDCs that have had success in economic development compared to those which have failed or at least not done as well? What approaches to development have been adopted in India, what effects have they had, and what are appropriate paths to follow?

Sometimes debates about issues of strategy have proceeded as if there are two or perhaps three alternative paths to development, for instance, a neoliberal strategy, a state-led autarkic strategy and some kind of a middle path. Such debates have been unnecessarily divisive and arguably failed to improve our understanding of the strengths and weaknesses of different strategies. Often the middle path has been forgotten. Rather than engaging in such broad debates, we may discuss strategies in terms of the questions about alternative paths to development mentioned in the introduction.

The State versus the Markets

Arguably the major debate regarding strategies of development has been about whether economic development is best promoted by harnessing the forces of the free market or through state involvement. In the early days of development economics after World War II, the experience with wartime controls and planning in more developed countries, the generally positive growth results of Soviet planned industrialization, the aspirations of the governments of newly independent LDCs, and the US's desire to promote development by providing foreign aid to LDC governments to confront the spectre of communism, led to a heavy reliance on the state as the driving force for development. This was attempted through extensive government ownership, planning, and regulation of the economy. After over two decades of the experience with this dirigiste development and its alleged poor results, the pendulum of opinion swung to favouring a market-oriented approach to development, a shift which received a boost from the spread of so-called neo-liberal policies which attempted to minimize the role of the state under Prime Minister Margaret Thatcher in the UK and President Ronald Reagan in the US. In India, a planned, state-led pattern of development, in which the public sector dominated the 'commanding heights' of the economy, was in place from the early 1950s to the mid-1970s but from then onwards, through the 1980s and especially from the early 1990s, India embarked on liberalizing reforms, which opened up the economy to the private sector, reduced government regulations, and virtually dismantled the earlier industrial licensing system or the 'license raj'.

The case for free markets is usually made in terms of Adam Smith's (1776) notion of the invisible hand and its modern mainstream neoclassical economics formalization in terms of the fundamental theorem of welfare economics, discussed in Chapter 3. According to this view, under certain conditions, a free market economy results in an efficient allocation of resources.

Free markets also promote productive efficiency by encouraging competition and make use of better information possessed by private individuals, who have better knowledge about what concerns them than does the state. State regulations were argued to distort free market incentives, result in inefficiencies, and promote corruption and activities which attempt to secure government favours rather than production and investment. Moreover, free markets expand economic freedoms while state intervention reduces individual freedom and interferes with the rights of individuals, for example, to private property.

The case for state intervention is made with the argument that the strict conditions that are required for the fundamental theorem of welfare, such as 'perfect' information and the absence of externalities, public goods, and large firms which can set prices, as discussed in Chapter 3, are unlikely to hold in real economies, especially in LDCs. Moreover, if the future is uncertain—rather than just risky in the sense that there are objectively calculable probabilities of future events—the economy can experience macroeconomic problems such as unemployment, inflation, and economic fluctuations, which can be corrected by suitable government policy. The government can also have better information about macro issues and, in fact, control the macro environment and overcome coordination problems like the one we encountered concerning the shoe factory in Chapter 3. The government can also reduce poverty and inequality, rather than focusing only on efficiency like the free market does, at least in terms of the fundamental theorem of welfare economics, and expand the functionings and capabilities of people, which can imply expanding freedoms and upholding certain rights (to education and adequate nutrition, for example), even though government restrictions may reduce certain freedoms and violate some rights.

The theoretical debates have been accompanied by controversies regarding interpretations of actual policy experiences around the world. The empirical case for free markets has been made by pointing to the general success of capitalist economies of Western Europe and the US and the demise of the Soviet Union. The case for government intervention is made by drawing attention to significant instances of government support for economic development in Western Europe and the US, and especially in Germany and Japan, and to the experiences of the Great Depression and the global financial crisis of the first decade of the twenty-first century, in which free markets are associated with economic decline and government intervention with recovery. Turning more specifically to LDCs in recent times, the experience of the East Asian newly-industrialized countries (NICs), such as South Korea and Taiwan, were initially interpreted as demonstrating the virtues of market-friendly strategies by the World Bank, among others, but later scholarship suggests the strong role of the state in these successful development efforts in the form of state-ownership of enterprises, government regulation and government allocation of credit to key industries (Amsden 1989; Wade 1990; Chang 2007). The poor performance of many LDCs, including India (Bhagwati 1993), has been laid at the door of state intervention. The more recent growth acceleration in China and India has also been attributed to free market reforms, although it has also been argued that the experiences of these countries included state intervention, which made possible the creation of an industrial base and technological upgrading and laid the foundations for the more recent growth accelerations. The growth successes are attributable to the fact

156

that they have liberalized guardedly and continue to have among the most state-interventionist economies among LDCs.

What these debates seem to overlook is the fact that the market and the state are not substitutes but are synergistic institutions which can strengthen the positive development effects of the other. The mainstream neoclassical approach to markets does not usually recognize the fact that the state and society need to provide markets with appropriate underpinnings so that private property rights are protected to some degree and contracts are enforced, and ensure that the excesses of market competition do not disrupt social stability, without which market economies will collapse (Polanyi 1944). Markets have many shortcomings, as discussed earlier, which open up the possibility that states can improve matters. But states can also create problems and not merely solve them, by promoting inefficiency and corruption and by furthering the goals of powerful groups in society at the expense of the less powerful, and ultimately at the expense of the country as a whole. The state can promote development if it can insulate itself from the pressures of these elites, provide incentives to relevant groups in society and, in return, demand appropriate results, and act in a pragmatic rather than doctrinaire manner, which destroys individual initiatives that can further development. In particular, the state can make use of market forces, among others, to discipline social groups to achieve desirable outcomes and provide incentives to those whose activities can promote development. There are no general formulae for the proper balance between the markets and the state and exactly how they can complement each other, since these depend on the economic, political, and social context of every country. A careful study and appraisal of these contexts, coupled with careful analytical thinking, is required.

Autarky versus Openness

A second major development debate is over whether LDCs should follow an autarkic or inward-looking development path or one that is outward oriented and seeks to increase links of the country with the global economy, through greater openness to international trade, foreign direct investment, and other forms of international capital flows. After World War II, there was a preference for a relatively inward-looking approach, which accompanied the general strategy of state-led industrialization. Many LDCs embarked on import-substituting industrialization, attempting to develop manufacturing industries under tariff barriers and import quotas. In addition to the goal of industrialization, these LDCs were arguably reacting to their colonial pasts, suspicious of the colonial pattern of trade in which they imported manufactured goods and exported primary products, and of transnational corporations which represented to them the new face of colonialism. Moreover, policymakers in LDCs seemed to believe that their prospects of increasing exports of primary and simple manufactured goods were limited (what has been called export pessimism), and foreign exchange shortages and the import needs of industrialization were seen as requiring foreign exchange controls and licensing. From roughly the same time, as the switch from state-led strategy to the market-friendly strategy occurred, the autarkic approach gave way to the more outward-oriented approach. Many explained the shift as occurring due to recognition of the inefficiencies and generally poor performance of the inward-looking approach, the exhaustion of the possibilities of import substitution, and the good performance of LDCs which were more outward oriented, such as the East Asian NICs. Since the shift in strategy generally involved the liberalization of trade and international capital inflows, according to many analysts, the switch from inward to outward orientation was seen as a switch from state-led approach to a free market one. However, the relationship between the two debates is not a simple one: as the East Asian experience shows, the outward-oriented strategy was pursued with active state intervention rather than through the free market and free trade approach.

India's approach reflected the general trend, although there were differences in timing and extent of change. India followed a highly protectionist trade policy in the early days after independence, in fact, pursuing what can be called a policy of self-reliance irrespective of cost. The move towards export promotion policies, for instance, by providing import tax concessions and other incentives to exporters, was started as early as the 1960s. Trade liberalization was under way by the 1980s and gathered steam from the 1990s. However, during the 1970s, India became more restrictive towards transnational corporations and while international capital flows were liberalized from the 1990s,

India's capital account is among the more regulated in the world.

The case for inward-looking development relies on the arguments discussed in Chapter 4 which point to the need for developing manufacturing industry to foster technological change and to diversify the economy away from primary production, for instance, due to the problems caused by deterioration of the terms of trade and volatility; the dangers of foreign direct investment caused by high profit repatriation, deleterious effects on domestic entrepreneurship and the inflow of inappropriate technology, and financial and foreign exchange instability caused by volatile international financial capital flows. The critics of such inward-looking development prefer an outward-oriented strategy because they argue that the promotion of exports increases the demand for domestic goods and brings in foreign exchange, exposes domestic producers (both import competing firms and exporting firms) to international competitive pressures, the absence of trade restrictions allows LDCs to produce according to their comparative advantage, which lies in labour-intensive goods resulting in rapid employment growth and reduction of poverty, less restrictive policies towards capital inflows results in the greater availability of foreign saving which can finance both domestic and foreign direct investment, and advanced foreign technology is brought in, in the case of FDI. It is claimed, using case studies and econometric analysis, that LDCs which are more open to trade and international capital flows tend to experience higher growth and lower levels of poverty. However, the robustness of the econometric studies has been questioned, and it is pointed out that although in some cases restrictions on trade and capital flows have had poor results, in others, as in the East Asian NICs, they have been more successful, and this success has been followed by some degree of trade and capital flow liberalization, which makes it seem that liberalization and economic success are causally related. An examination of the history of many of the more developed countries of today shows that these countries, including the UK, USA, Germany, and Japan, followed protectionist trade policies in the past to foster the development of their industries, and then become ardent free traders and champions of trade liberalization only after becoming more developed, attempting to kick away the ladder— in the words of the German economist Friedrich List, who supported protectionism during the early stages of his country's development—to prevent LDCs from following in their footsteps (Chang 2007).

The appropriate course to follow is neither an inward-looking strategy which indiscriminately imposes barriers on foreign trade and capital movements or an outward-oriented one which reduces these barriers, but a judicious combination of the two successful LDCs have used protectionist policies to give their nascent, relatively low-technology industries some breathing space to become internationally competitive, after which their governments have exposed them to foreign competition. While promoting the exports of these goods they have also provided tariff and other forms of protection to relative high-technology industries until some of them have been able to compete in international markets, and so on. These countries, including the East Asian NICs and, more recently, China, have sought to climb the technology ladder, and have benefited by exporting relatively high-technology goods. This is not a matter of choosing between import reduction and export expansion, as simple static trade theory models with full employment, balanced trade, and two goods seem to suggest. Not all countries can, of course, proceed along this path with equal success: in some cases the state is in no position, because it is too beholden to powerful domestic groups, to force large domestic firms to compete successfully in foreign markets, and others are too small and have small domestic markets to allow effective import substitution and the reaping of scale economies. Regarding foreign direct investment, countries that have been very hostile to transnational corporation and, indeed, dislodged them, as India did in the 1970s, paid a heavy technological price. However, other countries which experienced large amounts of FDI inflows have benefited by carefully directing it to sectors which could benefit most from foreign technology, and imposing restrictions on entry into some sectors (such as service sectors like retail and finance) in which the possibility of technology gains is minor and adverse effects of monopolization, profit repatriation and lack of government control is high, and require and induce the foreign firms to transfer technology to domestic firms as suppliers or as partners. Regarding other capital inflows, while it makes sense to encourage foreign borrowing with long maturity periods, it may be sensible to take steps to restrict short-term capital inflows and outflows with taxes and other restrictions. Countries that have successfully coped with volatile capital flows with minimum damage to growth and equity—for instance, during the global financial crisis of 2008—are those, including India, that have maintained a high a degree of government control over their financial sectors, maintained some control over international capital flows, and pursued anti-cyclical monetary and fiscal policies, maintaining high levels of aggregate demand with expansionary macroeconomic policies during financial crises involving capital outflows (Reddy 2011).

Growth versus Poverty, Inequality, and 'Social' Development

Early development economists and policymakers focused on achieving high rates of growth of income and production in LDCs. This is not to suggest that they ignored the problems of poverty and inequality, but they arguably believed that if the economy could be made to grow, poverty and even inequality would automatically and eventually decrease. Most countries, therefore, concentrated on increasing saving, investment, capital accumulation, and the rate of technological change, rather than focusing directly on poverty reduction. With the recognition of the fact that some LDCs, like Brazil, were experiencing rapid growth with rising inequality and little poverty reduction, and many others were experiencing neither significant increases in output nor reductions in poverty, from around the 1970s, there was a shift in focus from promoting growth to directly reducing poverty and inequality and addressing the problem of basic needs like food, health care, and shelter for the poor. This was done by providing cash assistance and increasing income opportunities for the poor, and with government policies that redistribute income to the poor. The success of some countries, such as Sri Lanka, Costa Rica, and Cuba, and states like Kerala in India, in terms of human development indicators such as health, education, and poverty reduction—without significant increases in income—has been recognized. Moreover, as we noted in Chapter 3, it has been argued that addressing the needs of the poor, such as basic health, education, and nutrition and reducing inequality promotes growth.

However, emphasizing either growth alone or poverty, inequality, and other 'social' development indicators without emphasizing growth is problematic. An increase in the growth rate may not have a positive effect on poverty and other 'social' indicators because output growth need not promote employment growth if labour productivity rises rapidly, and appropriate specific government policies may be required to affect the lives of the poor since market processes often exclude the poor. Attempts to reduce income poverty and improve health, education, and nutritional conditions, especially for the poor, may improve the conditions of the poor to a limited extent, but do little to make a large dent on the extent of poverty and reduce inequality, and is unlikely to promote sustained growth. Without sustained output and employment growth, improvements in education will have limited effects on the incomes of the poor and may even result in emigration abroad (though resulting increases in remittances can compensate to some extent, as discussed in Chapter 4). Moreover, without long-term and sustained economic growth, government finances can come under strain, especially after adverse external and internal political and economic shocks, which can make it difficult to sustain poverty-reduction and other social programmes. In other words, the recognition that economic development does not simply mean economic growth, as discussed in Chapter 2, does not imply that the best strategy for reducing poverty and inequality is by attacking them directly, without attempting to create conditions for sustained growth.

Macroeconomic versus Microeconomic Approaches

Macroeconomic approaches focus on indicators and policies at the macro or aggregate level, or at broad sectoral levels, while microeconomic approaches focus on interventions, both public and private, at the small—often village, or project—level. It is fair to say that early development economics focused mainly on the macroeconomic approach, on attempting to raise overall investment and saving rates, on inter-sectoral resource allocation, and on policy regarding trade and foreign direct investment. More recently, the focus seems to have become much more micro-oriented and involve funding and promoting small educational and health schemes, providing micro-loans to small enterprises, and the like. The shift has come about partly due to the limited success or even failure of some macro interventions, the growing importance of non-government organization and aid donor institutions that focus on small projects, and the growth of private charities and volunteering work which, understandably, look for greater personal involvement and results. In addition, the rise in popularity of evaluation techniques for small interventions (like randomized experiments which randomly select small projects to assess their effectiveness while ensuring that selected projects do not have some special advantages that make them more likely to fare well, for instance, by being located in more 'developed' areas), has favoured small projects. Moreover, micro approaches that do not significantly alter the status quo are less likely to be resisted by powerful groups who may focus on preventing more macro changes—involving, say, broad-based land reforms or fiscal redistribution—to maintain their power.

A micro focus has many advantages over a macro approach that neglects it. It can allow a more careful evaluation and understanding of how policy interventions work 'on the ground', so to speak. It is more capable of involving the poor themselves and obtaining a fuller understanding the needs and desires of the poor and what precisely motivates them (Banerjee and Duflo 2011), and is likely to involve the potential beneficiaries of 'development' initiatives in successfully implementing them. However, there are problems with neglecting macro issues and of expecting that the micro will simply translate into aggregate outcomes. Improving school attendance by teachers may certainly help to improve education, but it is not clear that it will help to increase employment and reduce poverty unless the students with education find jobs, for which we require that employment prospects grow. Further, policies that seem to 'work' at the micro level need not have the same result at the macro level because of what economists call fallacies of composition. For example, it may be relatively easy for a small increase in microcredit loans to increase incomes of a few self-employed entrepreneurs, but if there is a large increase in such loans, excessive competition among these small entrepreneurs who sell similar products will very likely fail to increase incomes for them. Moreover, some things that do not 'work' at the micro level may well 'work' if done on a larger scale, for instance, by generating sufficient aggregate demand or, along the lines emphasized by mainstream economists, positive externalities.

Primary Production, Manufacturing, and Services

As noted earlier, most early development economists stressed the importance of reducing the dependence of LDCs on primary production and developing the manufacturing sector for the reasons discussed in Chapter 3. Many LDCs adopted policies to promote the growth of their manufacturing sectors, sometimes even focusing on capital goods sectors. In part, as a result of these measures, manufacturing sectors in many LDCs expanded and the share of primary products in production and exports for many of them declined. The criticisms of this industrialization strategy grew louder over time, however, with the critics arguing that it led to inefficient industrialization, low employment generation (especially in the case of capital goods sectors), and a bias against agriculture, which resulted in food shortages, stagnant primary goods exports, and failure of significant poverty reduction (given that most of the poor lived in rural areas). While some argued that this was mainly the result of the early development economists' disdain for the agricultural sector as backward and traditional, others located the problem in the political economy of 'urban bias' resulting from the urban elite's desire to concentrate resources in cities to help themselves directly and indirectly by appeasing urban voters (Lipton 1977). Moreover, it has been argued that despite their primary sector orientation, some countries, like Canada, Australia, and Argentina, and some US states have done well in the past and others, including some oil-rich countries, Botswana and Chile, have more recently taken major strides by exporting primary and exhaustible products. As time went on development economists and policymakers began to focus more on the agricultural sector, with many countries experiencing productivity growth with the Green Revolution, and some countries pursuing policies to increase employment in rural areas, especially among the poor and sometimes in the non-agricultural sector.

In recent years some LDCs, including India have experienced a relative shrinkage of their manufacturing sectors with an expansion of their service sectors. The share of the service sector in GDP for India, for instance, was over 56 per cent in 2011, compared to 71 per cent in Japan, 78 per cent in the UK, and 79 per cent in the

USA (all in 2010). While some have welcomed this as reflecting the emergence of these countries as post-industrial economies following the path of successful more developed countries, others have viewed it as showing the service sector's role as a repository of those who cannot find employment in manufacturing and agricultural sectors and enter the informal service sector with low income and underemployment, and as evidence of deindustrialization which has adversely affected their technological dynamism. It should be noted that China's services share in GDP was 43 per cent and South Korea's was 58 per cent (despite the latter's much higher per capita income level).

Many of the protagonists of the debate on the strategy of industrialization take unwarrantedly extreme positions. Most of the reasons behind the early development economists' support of industrialization remain valid, including those about technological change and the external terms of trade. While it is true that there are countries and regions have achieved high levels of income and standards of living despite being primary-sector oriented, they can be seen essentially as appendages of larger national or international economies with which they were linked through migration, shared institutions and capital inflows. Moreover, though countries can experience economic improvements by exporting exhaustible primary resources, like copper (Chile), diamonds (Botswana), and oil (a number of petroleum-exporting countries), such improvements will be temporary unless the countries can successfully diversify their production structure by developing manufacturing. Further, even before the exhaustion of their resources, they are prone to terms of trade instability and political problems including civil and international wars. However, the industrialization argument does not require the neglect of other sectors like the agricultural one. Many of its proponents, in fact, did not recommend the neglect of agriculture: recall that Lewis (1954), who referred to that sector as a subsistence one rather than the modern capitalist sector, did discuss the possible dangers posed by rising food prices due to agricultural stagnation for industrial profits, capital accumulation, and growth. Indeed, as discussed in Chapter 3, there are many ways in which the agricultural sector contributes to economic growth and development, which means that the neglect of agriculture can be an important obstacle for economic development. Regarding the service sector, it should be recognized that all services are not the same. There are some services, like some education and information technology sectors, which can stimulate technological change, others, such as health care and most of education—which promote functionings and capabilities, while there are others, such as petty retailing and peddling, that can provide some income to the disguisedly unemployed and merely make a small dent on income poverty.

Supply versus Demand

Should development strategies seek to increase the supply of resources or the demand for them? This issue has been debated at both the micro and macro levels. At the micro level supply-siders [or those who Banerjee and Duflo (2011) call 'supply-wallahs'] argue that improvements in education and health, and increases in income and production, require building more schools and health clinics, and increasing the availability of inputs to producers, for instance high-yielding varieties of seeds, fertilizers, better technology for farmers, and that the increased availability of these resources will automatically increase their use. Demand-siders or demand-wallahs, on the other hand, argue that the way forward is to increase the demand for these resources and services, for instance, by providing incentives for families to send their children to school with cash incentives and school lunches and to farmers by raising food prices, and that when demand increases, supply will follow. At the macro level, the dominant mainstream approaches stresses the supply-side factors behind growth, such as increasing capital accumulation by encouraging saving and the effective supply of labour through technological improvements by encouraging research and development and the supply of education, while others stress the role of aggregate demand and recommend the use of expansionary fiscal and monetary policies, greater distributional equality to increase consumption demand, and measures to improve business confidence to encourage investment.

Somewhat paradoxically, at the micro level, those who are on the demand side are often in favour of reducing the role of the government to increase private incentives and those on the supply side favour government provisioning, while at the macro level, supply-siders usually seek to reduce the role of the state to provide incentives for more savings by reducing government expenditure and greater efficiency by reducing government regulation, while demand–siders often recommend more government intervention through expansionary macroeconomic policies and redistributive policies. It would be incorrect, however, to overemphasize these correspondences. Governments can provide incentives to increase demand at the micro level and private non–government organizations can provide health services. Governments can conduct research and development to increase supply at the macro level, and aggregate demand can be increased by encouraging private investment through the relaxation of burdensome industrial licensing policies.

In principle, both demand and supply sides are important at both micro and macro levels, although one of them may be worthy of more attention in some spheres of the economy and in some places and periods. In general, focusing only on the supply side at the micro level results in the wastage of resources, which people do not use or do not use effectively, while trying to increase demand is often unlikely to automatically increase supply, especially of an effective kind, through market forces or private charities. At the macro level, focusing only on the supply side by increasing government saving can result in stagnation due to the lack of aggregate demand, and attempts to improve technology can merely increase unemployment and underemployment. The tendency of many economists to relegate issues related to aggregate demand to the short run and maintaining tight limits on demand expansion in the longer run places undue faith in the self-adjusting character of markets, in which wage-price flexibility keeps the economy at the supply-determined growth in the long run. It forgets that the long-run is really an average of short run states of the economy. However, focusing only on the demand side can lead to inflationary pressures and mounting government debt unless supply-side bottlenecks are overcome, for instance, with the provision of infrastructure for industry and agriculture, and through improvements in education, skills, and work habits to meet increases in aggregate demand.

Resources versus Productivity

It has been claimed, perhaps with some justification, that early development economists and policymakers concentrated on growth through capital accumulation by focusing on increasing saving and investment and foreign saving (especially through foreign aid), rather than emphasizing the importance of efficiency and technological change. Critics of this approach (Easterly 2001) argue that the focus on resource accumulation led to a neglect of efficiency and incentives. As a result, high rates of capital accumulation did not result in high rates of growth because of the low levels of the efficiency and utilization of capital. A debate has raged on whether resource accumulation or productivity growth is more important, that has received added impetus from growth accounting, exercises which attempt to quantitatively identify the roles of the growth of the capital labour ratio and productivity growth using econometric techniques. Whether the rapid growth of the East Asian NICs was the result of factor accumulation or productivity growth has also been the subject of intense controversy (see Young 1995).

The sharp distinction between resource accumulation and productivity growth has been overdrawn. There are important complementarities between the two, and overemphasis on only one of them is likely to result in poor growth performance and even be self-defeating. Capital accumulation is a major driving force for technological change, for instance, due to scale economies, and what is called learning by doing, and technological change can be a major determinant of investment, to make use of new techniques embodied in machinery and to produce new goods. The existence of these relationships does not mean that specific measures to boost capital accumulation and productivity growth are not required: it is important to foster research organizations and favourable industrial relations to make technological change more responsive to investment, and to foster financial organizations and keep aggregate demand buoyant to make investment respond to new technological opportunities.

The Primacy of Institutions

A final debate concerns the role of institutions—which were discussed in Chapter 5—in development. While early development economists, with some exceptions, and policy makers did not emphasize institutions and instead focused on economic factors in a narrow sense, like saving, investment, and international capital flows, the importance of institutions and the need for institutional change is now widely acknowledged. Many mainstream economists—whose theories and models once ignored institutions—now refer to institutions as the 'fundamental' or 'deep' (as opposed to 'proximate') determinants of economic growth and development. Some go even further. Those who used to insist that it is essential to 'get the prices right' by reducing government regulations and ownership, now—in the wake of many failures of such neoliberal policies due to financial and economic crises—argue that one should first 'get the institutions right', for instance, by strengthening private property rights with laws and increasing the flexibility of markets, before pursuing neoliberal reforms.

Although these ideas raise a number of issues, here we note that the extreme views regarding institutions in the context of designing appropriate developed strategies—that institutions can be ignored or that institutional change of certain kinds must come first—are unwarranted. That institutions are important is now widely recognized, for instance, for effective government activity, for the proper functioning of markets, and indeed for basic social, economic, and political stability. More controversial is the desirability, feasibility, and necessity of prior institutional changes involving wholesale alterations in the legal environment (for instance, establishing clear private property rights) and social norms (for instance, those which lead to corrupt behaviour). First, on desirability, as discussed in Chapter 5, some of the broad changes often recommended—such as establishing clear private property rights—involve ideas that are difficult to define, can be compromised by changes involving social norms, and can have adverse consequences. Second, on feasibility, some of the changes are difficult to bring about and implement. For instance, constitutional changes can be blocked by powerful groups who perceive that their interests will be adversely affected by them (although there are some recent examples of countries, such as Venezuela, Bolivia, and Ecuador, that have made changes by forming Constituent Assembly through direct elections). Third, regarding necessity, social norms can be affected by changes in economic conditions and by small changes in policies and behaviour. For instance, norms regarding acceptable levels of corruption among some government employees (such as the police who are more likely to accept small bribes if they have low salaries) may be affected by income levels, and those regarding work habits are likely to depend on the effect of wages on motivations. Also, some norms and conventions can be altered by government actions, for instance, by taking advantage of what is called the status quo effect, stressed by behavioural economists, which induces a particular pattern of behaviour (such as increasing saving if employees are required to opt out of employee saving schemes—implying that they save if they do nothing—rather than opting into them). Participation rates of the poor (who are unable to read) in elections can be altered by simple innovations involving placing the pictures of candidates on ballots (Banerjee and Duflo 2011). Thus, prior institutional changes are not essential for improved development performance. There is, in fact, that little evidence to suggest that major growth spurts are preceded by major institutional changes (Rodrik 2007).

7

Conclusion

Although there is some debate on the question of appropriate pathways to economic development for LDCs such as India, one influential view—that can even be called the orthodox one—has it that the appropriate strategy to follow is to reduce government intervention in the economy to harness the forces of the free market and to open up the economy to global influences. Such a strategy, it is argued, encourages effort and creativity among people, and allows LDCs to learn from the best practices and draw on the resources that the world has to offer, and therefore allows them to become more efficient, achieve rapid growth in income and production per capita, and experience economic development. To be sure, some analysts and policymakers who support this general approach, recognize that the resultant process is likely to exclude the poor and increase inequality, so that market forces need to be supplemented with state efforts and assistance to reach out to the poor, by improving health and education, especially among the very poor. Even on this, some argue that the appropriate way to proceed is to create incentives among the poor rather than through state provisioning or even foreign aid.

Not only is this approach seen to be the appropriate one, but some argue that this is the approach that LDCs will, in fact, follow. Thus, economic development will occur inevitably and naturally in these countries, and sooner or later, all countries will become rich (or, broadly speaking, become economically developed). Lucas (2000), for instance, has argued that in the long run, actually by 2100, all countries will become rich, because latecomers will grow faster than more developed countries due to the fact that they can draw on the successful policy and institutional experiences (and resources and technology, already discussed in Chapter 4) of the latter.

Perhaps Lucas and others like him are being overly sanguine. Is it a simple matter for LDCs to develop following the example of the successful strategies of more developed countries? Although Lucas and others argue that the policies that successful countries of the past followed were free market ones, there is much evidence to suggest that they actually resorted to protectionist policies and combined state intervention with market competition. Moreover, it is not clear whether strategies that 'worked' in one context will necessarily succeed in others (due to differences not only in local conditions, but also because of changes in the nature of the global economy and power relations in it), and that the path of the more developed countries is a desirable one to follow (in view of its effects on the environment, happiness and, more recently, inequality within countries).

The orthodox view, which has been, and continues to be, espoused by the governments of most more developed countries, powerful international organizations like The World Bank, the International Monetary Fund, and the World Trade Organization, and has the support—inevitably with some variations in emphasis—of most mainstream economists, has been vehemently opposed by some who have gone to the extreme of becoming anti-globalization and anti-market, and have recommended strong state intervention and emphasis on communities rather than markets. The critics, however, are less powerful, represented in the governments of a few countries, and include some heterodox scholars who seem to look back wistfully to the earlier days of development economics with its advocacy on inward-looking and state-led development, although with a much stronger focus on the reduction of economic and social inequality.

If these orthodox and heterodox positions are extreme ones, is there a more sensible middle ground? While it is easy to espouse a more reasonable middle path, it is much more difficult to define it other than in the negative sense as one that avoids extremes. This book will have served its purpose if it has shed some light on issues that can help to formulate desirable pathways to economic development in particular contexts. These issues are complex ones. This is because of the intricacies involved in defining and measuring development as discussed in Chapter 2. It is also because there are many different obstacles to economic development, not just narrowly defined economic ones examined in Chapter 3, but also those rooted in the global economy, examined in Chapter 4 and in history, politics, and society as reviewed in Chapter 5.

What complicates matters further is that the relative importance of these obstacles is likely to vary over time and place. Given these complexities, we have argued in Chapter 6 that a sensible approach to choosing appropriate pathways to development requires the examination of a number of related but distinct debates in the analysis of economic development, rather than by seeking some sort of middle ground between overall alternative strategies. Choices have to be made by becoming aware of the alternative views and choosing wisely among them, taking into account detailed knowledge and understandings of specific contexts and conditions. A short book such as this one cannot examine such contextual details, let alone form clear conclusions about them, but can at least attempt to provide some guidance regarding the main questions to address.

In choosing desirable alternatives, it ought to be remembered that the economic development experience of the last half century or so seems to show that although there have been some improvements in terms of some indicators in many countries of the world, sustained long-term economic development is not easy to achieve. In terms of per capita income, apart

from some oil-rich countries, very few LDCs—South
Korea, Taiwan, and Singapore, for instance—have been
able to join the ranks of the more developed countries
(taking a minimum US$18,000 in PPP and nominal
dollar terms in 2011 as criterion of this status). By
many measures, there seems to be divergence in terms
of per capita income among the countries of the
world, suggesting an increase in the inequality among
nations (Milanovic 2008). Improvements in the earlier
part of the period have, in some cases such as some
Latin American countries, been reversed, especially in
the so-called lost decade of the 1980s, and in many
African countries growth performance has often been
poor. China and, to some extent, India, have experienced high rates of economic growth, but they were
ranked 96th and 126th in PPP terms, in terms of per
capita GDP in 2011, with 50 countries having per capita income in excess of US$18,000. To be sure, major
improvements have taken place in many countries in
terms of basic health and education indicators, as well
as in terms of the reduction of absolute income poverty,
and there has been convergence in terms of these indicators among countries. However, it is arguable that in
a global economy such improvements, while reducing

189

human suffering to some extent in many parts of the world, are unlikely to lead to sustained long-run economic development, especially in view of the increases in income inequality within many countries, including China and India.

Given that only a few countries have achieved success in terms of economic development according to a broad range of indicators in the last half century, it is tempting to conclude that luck is of great importance. As the experiences of the recent developers like South Korea and Taiwan suggest, luck has something to do with it, given their geopolitical importance (which induced the US to help them with foreign aid and market access for their products) and political economy conditions as discussed in Chapter 6. However, it can be argued that there are ways of increasing the chances of favourable outcomes by proceeding along the lines outlined in this book.

We conclude by briefly noting two major barriers to this. First, as discussed especially in chapters 4 and 5, there are powerful groups in the global economy and within LDCs that can severely constrain the ability of these countries to embark on appropriate paths to economic development. For instance, more developed

countries like the US and international agencies
have imposed trade and capital account liberalization
on LDCs which have often had damaging effects
on their economies, and forced the latter to adopt
stringent intellectual property rights protection, which
arguably make technology transfers more difficult.
Powerful elites within LDCs have blocked desirable
policy and institutional changes, such as land reforms
in agriculture. While these constraints often impose
major barriers, as mentioned in Chapter 5, there are
situations in which the state can find itself relatively
insulated against them, and can bring about changes,
especially those that take small steps. In addition, it
is sometimes in the enlightened self-interest of the
powerful groups to accept such changes, since they can
collectively benefit from them. Moreover, some of the
views which find support from powerful elites may
arise not in narrow self-interest, but because of their
limited knowledge and understanding of the problems
faced by, and the perspectives of, the less powerful, a
situation that can be altered with some effort. Finally,
power is exercised not simply through political means,
but also by influencing ideas, for instance, about the
benefits of free trade and free international capital

flows. If these ideas are questioned and found to be wanting, the constraints can weaken.

Second, the discussion of economic development in the policy space seems to be dominated by economics, which, in turn, is dominated by mainstream neoclassical economics. Although it is not clear what exactly mainstream neoclassical economics signifies, two of its major characteristics appear to be the insistence that theoretical analysis needs to be based on the optimizing behaviour of agents and the strong preference for 'rigorous' mathematical analysis involving theory and empirical analysis. This is not the place for a thorough discussion of the strengths and weaknesses of this approach but a few comments on them may be relevant, in view of its implications for the question of how the problems of economic development are best analysed. The optimizing approach has undoubtedly increased our understanding of many problems plaguing LDCs, through the careful examination of the objectives and beliefs of, and constraints and environments faced by, individuals. However, by insisting that all analyses needs to be based on it, the approach has arguably, and perhaps unwittingly, characterized people and the economy in particular ways. People are

192

seen as 'rational' (an ambiguous term) rather than, as behavioural economists have found from their study of actual behaviour, as making consistent 'mistakes'. Markets are seen as reasonably well functioning ones, with only a few 'distortions' that lead to market failures, in order to make models based on the optimizing model tractable; this arguably leads to an overly optimistic view of the benefits of markets since removing the distortions seems to be relatively easy. The emphasis on mathematical analysis arguably turns attention away from complex phenomenon that are difficult to formalize with mathematical models or to model them in simplistic ways, leads to a tendency to 'apply' models to particular countries without careful reflection, and leads to an overemphasis on quantification and what seems to be easily quantifiable, and formal techniques, rather than to a focus on understanding the main characteristics of particular contexts and how individuals and groups behave within them. Although the optimizing approach, mathematical modelling, and the econometric analysis of available data can certainly contribute to our understanding of economic development, there is also the need for alternative approaches that study actual behaviour, understand the needs of people, especially the less powerful, and that examine the nature, implications, and dynamics of specific structures in LDCs. This also requires greater attention to anthropology, psychology, history, politics, and sociology, in addition to economics narrowly defined. Although there is some evidence that a few mainstream economists are going in this direction, there is still a long way to go.

Bibliography

Acemoglu, Daron and James Robinson. *Why Nations Fail: The Origins of Power, Prosperity, and Poverty*. Crown Business, 2012.

Amsden, Alice H. *Asia's Next Giant: South Korea and Late Industrialization*. Oxford and New York: Oxford University Press, 1989.

—————. *The Rise of 'The Rest'*. Oxford and New York: Oxford University Press, 2001.

Bagchi, Amiya Kumar. *Perilous Passage: Mankind and the Global Ascendancy of Capital*. Lanham, USA: Rowman & Littlefield, 2005.

Banerjee, Abhijit V. and Esther Duflo. *Poor Economics*. New York: Public Affairs, 2011.

Banerjee, Abhijit V., Paul J. Gertler, and Maitreesh Ghatak. 'Empower-ment and Efficiency: Tenancy Reform in West Bengal.' *Journal of Political Economy* 110, no. 2 (2002): 239–80.

Bardhan, Pranab. *Political Economy of Development in India*. Oxford and New York: Oxford University Press, 1999 (1984).

Bell, Martin, and Keith Pavitt. 'Accumulating Technological Capability in Developing Countries.' Proceedings of the World Bank Annual Conference on Development Economics, 1993, pp. 257–81.

Bhagwati, Jagdish. *India in Transition: Freeing the Economy*. Oxford and New York: Oxford University Press, 1993.

————. *In Defense of Globalization* (with a new afterword). USA: Oxford University Press, 2007.

Boldrin, Michele, and David K. Levine. *Against Intellectual Monopoly*. Cambridge, UK: Cambridge University Press, 2008.

Bulmer-Thomas, V. *The Economic History of Latin America since Independence*. Cambridge: Cambridge University Press, 1994.

Chang, Ha-Joon. *The Bad Samaritans*. Bloomsbury Press, 2007.

Chua, Amy. *World on Fire: How Exporting Free Market Democracy Breeds Ethnic Hatred and Global Instability*. New York: Anchor, 2004.

David, Paul A. 'Clio and the Economics of QWERTY.' *American Economic Review* 75, no. 2 (1985): 332–7.

Diamond, Jared M. *Guns, Germs, and Steel*. New York: Norton, 1997.

Dutt, Amitava Krishna. *Growth, Distribution and Uneven Development*. Cambridge, UK: Cambridge University Press, 1990.

Dutt, Amitava Krishna. 'Post-Keynesianism and the Role of Aggregate Demand in Development Economics.' In *The Oxford Handbook of Post-Keynesian Economics*, edited by Geoff C. Harcourt and Peter Kreisler. Oxford: Oxford University Press, 2013.

Dutt, Amitava Krishna and Jaime Ros (eds). *International Handbook of Development Economics* (two volumes). Cheltenham, UK: Edward Elgar, 2008.

Easterly, William R. *The Elusive Quest for Growth: Economists' Adventures and Misadventures in the Tropics*. Cambridge, Massachusetts, USA: MIT Press, 2001.

Escobar, Arturo. *Encountering Development: The Making and Unmaking of the Third World*. Princeton, New Jersey: Princeton University Press, 2011.

Evans, Peter B. 'Predatory, Developmental, and Other Apparatuses: A Comparative Political Economy Perspective on the Third World State.' *Sociological Forum* 4, no. 4 (1989): 561–87.

————. *Embedded Autonomy: States and Industrial Transformation*. Princeton, New Jersey, USA: Princeton University Press, 1995.

Hirschman, Albert O. *The Strategy of Economic Development*. New York: Norton, 1958.

Keynes, John Maynard. *The General Theory of Employment, Interest and Money*. London: Macmillan, 1936.

Kohli, Atul. *State-directed Development: Political Power and Industrialization in the Global Periphery*. Cambridge, UK: Cambridge University Press, 2004.

Lal, Deepak. *The Hindu Equilibrium: India c. 1500 BC–2000 AD.* Oxford: Oxford University Press, 2004.

Lewis, W. Arthur. 'Economic Development with Unlimited Supplies of Labor.' *Manchester School* 22, no. 2 (1954): 139–91.

Lipton, Michael. *Why Poor people Stay Poor: A Study of Urban Bias in World Development.* London: Temple Smith, 1977.

Lucas, Robert E. 'Some Macroeconomics for the 21st Century.' *Journal of Economic Perspectives* 14, no. 1 (2000): 159–68.

Mahalanobis, Prasanta C. 'Some Observations on the Process of Growth of National Income.' *Sankhya* 12, no. 4, September (1953): 307–12.

Milanovic, Branko. *Worlds Apart: Measuring International and Global Inequality.* Princeton, New Jersey: Princeton University Press, 2008.

Morishima, Michio. *Why has Japan 'Succeeded'?* Cambridge, UK: Cambridge University Press, 1982.

Morris, Morris David. 'Values as an Obstacle to Economic Growth in South Asia: An Historical Survey.' *Journal of Economic History* 27, no. 4 (1967): 588–607.

Nair, Kusum. *Blossoms in the Dust: The Human Factor in Indian Development.* New York: Praeger, 1962.

Nurkse, Ragnar. *Problems of Capital Formation in Underdeveloped Countries and Patterns of Trade and Development.* Oxford: Oxford University Press, 1967.

Olson, Mancur. *The Logic of Collective Action: Public Goods and the Theory of Groups.* Cambridge, Massachusetts, USA: Harvard University Press, 1965.

Ostrom, Elinor. *Governing the Commons: The Evolution of Institutions for Collective Action.* Cambridge, UK: Cambridge University Press, 1990.

Polanyi, Karl. *The Great Transformation: The Political and Economic Origins of our Time.* New York: Farrar and Rinehart, 1944.

Prebisch, Raul. *The Economic Development of Latin America and Its Principal Problems.* New York: Economic Commission for Latin America, Department of Economic Affairs, United Nations, 1950, pp. 1–59.

Ray, Debraj. *Development Economics.* Princeton, New Jersey: Princeton University Press, 2011.

Reddy, Y.V. *Global Crisis, Recession and Uneven Recovery.* Hyderabad: Orient Blackswan, 2011.

Rodrik, Dani. *One Economics, Many Recipes: Globalization, Institutions, and Economic Growth.* Princeton, USA: Princeton University Press, 2007.

Ros, Jaime. *Development Theory and the Economics of Growth.* Ann Arbor, Michigan, USA: University of Michigan Press, 2001.

Rosenstein-Rodan, Paul N. 'Problems of Industrialisation of Eastern and South-eastern Europe.' *Economic Journal* 53, no. 210/211 (1943): 202–11.

Sen, Amartya. *Development as Freedom.* New York: Anchor Books, 1999.

Singer, Hans. 'The Distribution of Gains between Investing and Borrowing Countries.' *American Economic Review* May (1950): 473–85.

Smith, Adam. *An Inquiry into the Nature and Causes of the Wealth of Nations*, 2 volumes. New York and London: Oxford University Press, 1978 (1776).

Stiglitz, Joseph. *Globalization and Its Discontents*. New York: W.W. Norton, 2002.

Taylor, Lance. *Structuralist Macroeconomics: Applicable Models for the Third World*. New York, USA: Basic Books, 1983.

The World Bank. *World Development Report 2006, Equity and Development*. Oxford: The World Bank and Oxford University Press, 2005.

Thirlwall, Anthony P. *Economics of Development: Theory and Evidence*. Basingstoke, UK and New York, USA: Palgrave-Macmillan, 2011.

Wade, Robert. *Governing the Market: Economic Theory and the Role of Government in East Asian Industrialization*. Princeton, New Jersey: Princeton University Press, 1990.

Weber, Max. *The Protestant Ethic and the Spirit of Capitalism*. Translated by Talcott Parsons. New York: Scribner, 1930.

Young, Alwyn. 'The Tyranny of Numbers: Confronting the Statistical Realities of the East Asian Growth Experience.' *Quarterly Journal of Economics* 110, no. 3 (1995): 641–80.

Index